Life as a Psychologist

Life as a Psychologist

Career Choices and Insights

GERALD D. OSTER

Westport, Connecticut
London

Library of Congress Cataloging-in-Publication Data

Oster, Gerald D.
    Life as a psychologist : career choices and insights / Gerald D. Oster.
        p.   cm.
    Includes bibliographical references and index.
    ISBN 0–275–98598–9 (alk. paper)
    1. Psychology—Vocational guidance.   I. Title.
    BF76.088   2006
    150.23'73—dc22   2006006635

British Library Cataloguing in Publication Data is available.

Library of Congress Catalog Card Number: 2006006635
ISBN: 0–275–98598–9

First published in 2006

Praeger Publishers, 88 Post Road West, Westport, CT 06881
An imprint of Greenwood Publishing Group, Inc.
www.praeger.com

Printed in the United States of America

∞™

The paper used in this book complies with the
Permanent Paper Standard issued by the National
Information Standards Organization (Z39.48–1984).

10 9 8 7 6 5 4 3 2 1

This book is dedicated to my mother

Estelle Oster

An unpaid, but nevertheless professional caregiver
to her community

Without whose emotional support I would not
have had the opportunity to live my

"Life as a Psychologist"

Contents

Chapter 4 ∼ The Ins and Outs of Graduate School 73

Chapter 5 ∼ Pioneers in Psychology 93

Preface

Writing this book had many beginnings. I had been transitioning from working for over twenty years as a clinician in state hospitals and residential treatment centers, and more recently at the University of Maryland Medical School, to a more "serene" existence in private practice and consultation. To me, this meant less driving, fewer administrative demands, and no required meetings. But with this change in life direction came many thoughts of missed colleagues, less structured time, and diminished motivation to stay current in the field—probably all musings that pass through someone approaching retirement age.

To overcome this beginning malaise, I began attending a writers' group of psychology colleagues. Through this experience of lamenting about time commitments, constantly changing demands in life, and the altering movements within psychology, I decided that engaging in another project would focus my energy and efforts. Because I had written many books over the years on such topics as teenage depression, child therapy and assessment, and the clinical uses of drawings, I thought that it was time to reflect on my own "Life as a Psychologist." I solicited feedback from my writers' group and then asked former colleagues and other psychologists throughout the United States to share their personal meanings and adventures in pursuit of their professional identities.

With this framework in mind, I did what I do best these days—I logged onto the internet! The cyberspace environment allowed me to readily contact a broad range of psychologists to ask them for stories and contributions. I was initially astounded and appreciative that they were so readily available to my queries and that their responses were so overwhelmingly positive. I discovered many people eager to share their lives and perspectives on their chosen profession. That so many well-known psychologists were easily contacted and excited to participate both humbled and pleased me. It may be that psychology is a profession of giving back; in this case to the next generation of students. Thus, I received much correspondence from professors, clinicians, textbook writers, and others for whom the discipline of psychology has provided immense meaning and given considerable skills to navigate the world at large.

To this end, I found individuals in diverse fields: one who spent many of his professional years as a psychologist in the military, and another who devoted his passions and professional training promoting peaceful world coexistence. I located "pioneers" of psychology who have paved the way for future generations by exploring new paradigms in describing child development and personality theories. I solicited contributions from well-known professors who offered fascinating tidbits of why they chose psychology as a career. I also obtained comments from beginning teachers who are finding that psychology has helped them balance their lives between work and family, as well as answer many questions about themselves, their interests, and their world. Trying to find a diverse group who would offer views of their work led me to people who have gained invigorating vocations outside the typical career in psychology, such as becoming presidents of universities, running for local political offices, or working within departments outside of mainstream psychology (e.g., public health or women's studies). I also found active counselors and clinicians who were willing to reveal which turning points in their lives made them become professional caretakers.

In recruiting psychologists to share their stories and reflections, I initially contacted friends, friends of friends, and former professors of mine. From these willing participants, I expanded my search on the internet to a broad scope of those individuals who could show what a psychology degree can bring to a fulfilling and meaningful career. I looked across the country for easily accessible websites. I sent e-mails to anyone who seemed to have diverse interests. The responses were equally varied—from short statements (as I initially requested) to very long life stories. Even though some individuals declined to share their views or their stories, most people contacted were eager to write personal reflections. All responses were welcome, and most remain unchanged.

Hearing from psychology luminaries I had known only through their books or research articles made me ecstatic! I was also thrilled to hear from well-known personalities, even when they politely turned me down. Of course, I was thankful to all the people who contributed to this book by willingly offering details of their personal lives and careers. Although not a systematic study of psychology, this volume provides a broad framework for students interested in pursuing psychology as their life's work and through the variety of interests explored in the stories gives them a view of what is possible when commitment and passion are involved.

In their memoirs, these contributors demonstrate how their chosen discipline of psychology has enriched their lives and has challenged them in maintaining their focus, dreams, and endeavors throughout their lengthy and active schedules. The voices heard in these pages offer poignant views about psychology as a life work, provide memories of past working conditions with collegial conversations and struggles, and relive how family life and life's travails have affected the everyday balance of work and commitment to others.

It is essential for today's students to have a benchmark to reflect on psychology's past in their role as students, as well as a mirror to their future as professionals and as members of their surrounding community. For the psychologists involved in writing their thoughts for this volume, it has been a time of reflection and of giving back to their chosen field. In their stories they share life as graduate students within different departments, in schools, and through varying decades in psychology's history. They note turning points in their careers and mention the mentors who had major impacts on their lives.

Choosing a direction after graduate school is always crucial, and the contributors to this book offer glimpses of how they decided upon their respective life paths. They speak not only of personal options but also of compromises they made to accommodate significant others in their lives. They also share why they sought postgraduate experiences in well-known academic centers in the metropolitan cities or preferred rural lifestyles as they embarked on their life's journeys.

Today's students need this feedback from teachers, supervisors, and other successful professionals. The remarks in this book offer students insights into a profession that is constantly changing and requires of its members adaptability in seeking personal growth and making practical career choices. Readers will benefit wholeheartedly from examining firsthand the life experiences shared in this volume, in addition to seeing what everyday jobs in psychology are really like.

These reflections combine an enriched understanding of life and work. The contributors—all consummate professionals—reveal their lifestyles, the ups and downs of the life decisions they have made throughout, what events drew them into the field, and how they established themselves over time. They also offer practical advice based on their years of experience and the roles they have developed for themselves. Hearing from these experienced individuals will offer exciting portrayals of careers on campuses, in clinical practices, and within professional organizations. These stories also demonstrate alternative roles in psychology where applied research and adaptable skills are the requirement.

This book will take the reader in many directions. The shared stories provide unique perspectives on meaningful lives and careers within psychology. Students who are deciding, or who have already made the decision, to seek psychology as a major and potential profession will be pleased to hear that this directional choice can meet many of their personal needs. Reading these stories will also give students a variety of ideas about applying their skills in many possible directions. Knowing that psychology can answer personal as well as societal questions allows students the opportunity to see themselves wearing many hats in their lives, in addition to discovering themselves at a deeper level. Mainly, the reader will learn from these stories that psychology can be a productive, valued, stable, and even lucrative career choice. The discipline itself allows for experimentation, creativity, and intellectual challenges that make each day fruitful. Oh, yes, it is hard work; but rarely does one discipline provide so much to stimulate the soul!

The magic of this book is in the sharing. Many stories begin by contributors' mentioning their mentors. Regardless of professional choice, having a personal advisor and model always seems to be the key to selecting a life direction. Someone either excited a student or colleague about a research or clinical problem or just reached out. The many psychologists who reflected on their experiences understand this process. Through their daily lectures, interactions with clients, contacts with the community, or individual work with students or other people they hope to connect with other people. Realizing the continuity of life, they want to assist the new generation of scholars and helpers, though these may face many different demands and have many different visions of their world.

Readers of this book are sure to be amazed at the variety of practitioners in psychology. Within this discipline many have become politicians, writers, or consultants for sports teams and businesses. Academia has also produced a bevy of brilliant researchers and teachers, many of whom have been eager to share their stories here. Outside the academic sphere, psychologists have generalized their knowledge to areas of behavioral medicine, gerontology, and law. When it seems there are few new jobs, psychologists appear at the forefront in stretching the limits, in using their skills to secure positions within different arenas, such as television and other media. And of course, applied technology certainly considers the background of psychologists as central to designing new paths to bridging the gap between human needs and safety within the interface of computers and other machines.

In my own case, at age seventeen I (like many of you, I am sure) was not absolutely certain of my career direction. I took a step here and a misstep there along life's path. I resembled the nontraditional student in taking a while to find myself (easier to do in the 1960s and 1970s), but the extra time gave me both the motivation and the focus to work extra hard once I had chosen a specific career. This delay taught me to worry less about struggling at new pursuits or attempting different roles. The richness of my background within psychology supported this foundation and allowed me to entertain many new ideas with my newly acquired skills. Having had the opportunities to work at the highest levels of research at the National Institute of Mental Health, coordinate internship programs, perform everyday clinical work within hospitals and outpatient clinics, write professional articles and books, present seminars, and conduct workshops, I have had a full and active professional life. And my decision to pursue psychology (even at the "late" age of twenty-five) was a good choice and the right one!

So, thank you, Psychology, for making many lives that much richer and in return for making the world certainly a more interesting place to live, work, and provide a secure future for everyone.

Acknowledgments

Over the years, I have interacted with many people—professors, fellow graduate students, professional colleagues, and of course those individuals who confront me on a daily basis with their problems and who seek direction within our developing relationship. All have impacted me to varying degrees in my growth and I owe them much credit in my continuing work.

When I first decided to become a psychologist (several years after graduating with a degree in sociology), I reentered school at Florida International University in Miami where I was greatly influenced by two professors, Gordon Finley, Ph.D., and Barry Crown, Ph.D. Their courses in child development and humanistic psychology opened my eyes to possibilities and provided me with a directional path. Next I entered a master's degree program at Middle Tennessee State University where I had the fortune of not only being taught by passionate and creative teachers, such as Robert Prytula, Ph.D., but I also had the opportunity to remain an extra year to develop diagnostic and testing skills at a juvenile delinquent center headed by exceptional clinicians, such as Jay Gorban, Ph.D., and Denis Lewandowski, Ph.D.

My journey toward a doctoral degree continued at Virginia Commonwealth University in Richmond where I had the good luck of befriending so many energetic, thoughtful, caring, and fun-loving individuals. My first mentor, Robert Hamm, Ph.D., provided me with a balance between diligent researcher (taking care of his rat lab) and competitive recreation (racquetball). My next advisor, Iris Parham, Ph.D., extended my interest into the fields of gerontology and life-span development, and provided me with many professional opportunities and financial support. Later influences included Marilyn Erickson, Ph.D., who accepted me as one of her child clinical students, and Stewart Gabel, M.D., with whom I had the fortune to collaborate with in clinical settings, and who introduced me to the world of book writing.

Of course, my friends in graduate school and those later work colleagues with whom I have shared so many interesting exchanges throughout the years also deserve much praise. Settings such as the Child Psychiatry Center in Philadelphia, the Thomas B. Finan Center in Cumberland, Maryland, the Regional Institute for Children and Adolescents in Rockville, the Walter P. Carter Center and University of Maryland Medical School in Baltimore, and Montgomery General Hospital in Olney have all provided me with memorable experiences.

In writing this book, I also need to recognize many talented people at Greenwood Publishing Group and Praeger Press for their support, ideas, and timely editing. These include: Debora Carvalko, Senior Acquisitions Editor, and her editorial staff, Lisa Pierce, Kathleen Knakal, and Erin Ryan, as well as Rebecca Homiski, production editor at Westchester Book Services. I also want to mention a student, Jordana Koslovsky, who assisted me in locating information on various psychologists across the country. Certainly, I also wish to acknowledge the many talented and professional psychologists who make up the bulk of the book and who were so kind in offering their voices to the readership. Further, I would like to thank the people in my book writing club whose fresh insights and stimulation allowed me to pursue the idea of this book, and my community band members who give me another outlet to channel my interests.

Finally, I need to thank the continuing encouragement of my immediate family. My wife, Jo Warwick, who now is working full time as a special education teacher, and my children, Aaron Oster, age nineteen, who has ventured into college with the hope of pursuing a career in sports writing and broadcasting, and Corriane Oster, age sixteen, who has discovered her passion through musical theater. So far neither is headed into a direction of psychology—but who knows, that may change, and if not, that's certainly okay.

CHAPTER 1

Discovering Psychology

WHY STUDY PSYCHOLOGY?

Psychology is the systematic study of how animals, and particularly humans, perceive, interpret, and think about their world (Morris & Maisto, 2004). Through scientific rigor, psychologists attempt to construct theories and experimental models to explain every aspect of behavior—both simple and complex, internal and external, observable and inferred (Myers, 2003). For example, psychologists may investigate why people smoke or how mechanisms in the brain affect learning. They apply principles of learning discovered in the animal laboratory to explain a wide range of problems in personality and social behavior. In this manner, Dr. Martin Seligman of the University of Pennsylvania and his colleagues were able to demonstrate how animals could "learn to be helpless" and then generalize these principles to the study of clinical depression (Peterson, Maier, & Seligman, 1995). Other psychologists have explored the relationships between sleep and dreams, how people can abuse their authority, how it is possible to teach a chimpanzee sign language, how different parts of the brain have unique functions, and how environments can be altered to change behavior.

Compared to other sciences, the study of psychology is relatively young, about 150 years old (Lahey, 2003). Psychology examines subject matter from biology to sociology, exploring the structures and functions of living organisms, as well as how groups live in society. Psychologists study the intricate relationships between brain and behavior, in addition to examining the complexities between the external world (or the environment) and behavior. Like other scientists, psychologists carefully pursue the rigors of scientific methods by using careful observation, developing creative experiments, and understanding and disseminating the resulting statistical analyses.

Psychology is a vast and intriguing field with many applications in the workforce. Its discoveries and research in each of its subparts are usually related to work in other areas. The science and discipline of psychology is generally divided into a number of separate specialties with overlapping areas. What one person finds in one area or in one experiment can often generalize into resolving other problems that may appear in other settings. While the main professional organization of psychology (the American Psychological Association, or APA) has over forty divisions that connect like-minded individuals to focus on one theme (for example, the division of peace psychology), the discipline of psychology primarily focuses on six or seven main entities. These include sensation, perception, and psychophysics; experimental; developmental; personality; psychopathology; and social and environmental categories within psychology.

SENSATION, PERCEPTION, AND PSYCHOPHYSICS

Sensation, perception, and psychophysics together form a subfield in psychology. Questions that are asked within this subdiscipline may include: How do we see color? How can we manage to follow one conversation at a party when others are going on in the background? Why does a tall person look about the same height whether he is 10 feet away or 100 feet away? Generally, this area of psychology studies how organisms receive and interpret the information around them. It attempts to describe how the sense organs work, what stimuli they respond to, how this stimulation is translated in the brain into our physical experiences, and the relationship between psychological and physical stimulation. It is probably the oldest-studied area in modern psychology, dating back to the middle of the nineteenth century.

EXPERIMENTAL PSYCHOLOGY

These questions are asked within the subfield experimental psychology: Why do we forget? How do we remember one piece of information from all the others stored in our memory? What are emotions, and how do we best describe them? How do we solve problems? How do children learn to speak in grammatically correct sentences? Experimental psychology covers many topics, among them learning, memory, motivation, and emotions. Most of the undergraduate years in psychology are spent studying questions in these categories and developing applicable principles.

Life Span Development

Life span development is a branch of psychology that focuses on the maturation process and its maintenance and decline throughout the life cycle. Questions about child rearing, stages of child development, moral development, descriptions of the adolescent years, mid-life direction, and the issues of aging all fall under this field. Theorists and researchers combine their skills to explore the changes of growth and the impact that physical, psychological, and environmental changes have on people throughout their lives.

Personality

Personality is the area in psychology that explores such facets as temperament, stereotypes, kinds of attitudes, and preferences in everyday behavior. It also concerns the interrelationships among various parts of an individual's structure, as well as the interdynamics of how people function. How situational variables, rather than an individual's own style, affect behavior also produces many valid investigations.

Psychopathology, Abnormal Psychology, and Clinical Psychology

Psychopathology, abnormal psychology, and clinical psychology are perhaps the subdivisions in psychology that are most intriguing to the general population. Explanations of mental illness, analyses of criminal behavior, or treatments for a myriad of conditions are discussed at length within the media. Thus, many people come to study psychology to learn about these extreme conditions and, in turn, to learn a little bit about themselves. Studies in this field concentrate on disturbances to everyday functioning, such as depression, anxiety, phobias, and compulsive behaviors. Theories abound to explain extreme behavior, and much study involves the theories of attachment, social learning, and family systems, as well as clinical practices that attempt to use these models to solve individual and societal problems.

Social and Environmental Psychology

Questions that stimulate persons doing research in social and environmental psychology may include these: How can you change someone's attitude? Why does advertising work? What makes people like or love each other? How does noise affect us? Are cities unhealthy places to live? Topics in the study of these subdisciplines of psychology focus on the study of social groups, interpersonal behavior, such as aggression, and people's reactions to their environments.

PSYCHOLOGY AS A SCIENTIFIC DISCIPLINE

One question that people often ask psychologists is why there has to be a scientific field devoted to studying something that everyone already knows so much about. It is certainly true that an unusual characteristic of the field of psychology is that everyone is to some extent an expert on the subject. Most of us have no direct experience with chemical reactions, laser beams, actions of drugs, genetics, or even the internal workings of our bodies. We come to the fields of chemistry, physics, medicine, and biology with few pre- conceptions, we are ready to be told "the truths."

In contrast, we all have considerable experience with the subject matter of psychology. We spend our lives interacting with people, observing them and ourselves, and naturally have gathered all sorts of information about how we and others function. If we did not have this information, we would be unable to get along with the world around us. We know that when we go from a dark room into the sunlight or the other way around, our eyes take a while to "get used" to the change; that we like activities for which we are rewarded; and that the longer we have gone without eating, the hungrier we are and the more we will eat. We also have learned that people usually like other peo- ple who are similar to them; that we get angry and aggressive when someone annoys us; that we have dreams that we cannot remember clearly; and that we are often influenced by advertisements and political campaigns. Anyone who is in college has naturally learned a great deal about human behavior without ever studying it scientifically. The knowledge gives students of psychology a big head start because much of what they will encounter in the courses are already familiar, "sound right," and can be fitted into their own experiences.

However, personal experience also causes trouble because not everything we think we know about human behavior is correct. Systematic research often shows that common assumptions about how we act are wrong—that intuitions and day-to-day observations lead to false conclusion. Indeed, that is why there needs to be a systematic study of psychology. We must discover which of our intuitions are correct, and also, of course, learn other facts about ourselves that do not appear intuitive at all. This does not mean that our personal observations are always wrong—it does mean that systematic study is necessary to find out when they are right. And that is what psychology provides!

Through the study of human development; animal learning; the biological basis of behavior, sensation, and perception; personality theory; abnormal behavior; and experimental design, the discipline of psychology creates a solid foundation for many professional pursuits. Employers are especially interested in the high level of skills that psychology majors bring to potential jobs given their exposure to collecting, analyzing, and interpreting data combined with their understanding of personal and interpersonal dynamics. They view psychology majors as both intelligent and adaptable to filling many roles within various organizations and businesses.

And job satisfaction among psychologists is very high. Most psychologists say they love their work and find great meaning in much of what they do daily. Many of the stories in this book cite the extraordinary variety of responsibilities encountered daily and the flexibility in schedules as main advantages to careers in psychology. Psychologists have also viewed the changing world positively and see many expanding roles for themselves in an evolving workplace. This fast-paced development is highly visible from their collaboration with medical personnel, in addition to the advent of computer technology. Mostly, psychologists are committed to helping people manage the rhythms of daily life, as well as assisting society to adapt to new stresses and to novel ideas.

In correspondence with Dave Myers, Ph.D., who has written best-selling textbooks for social and introductory psychology classes, commented on lessons he learned in discovering psychology as his life's work.

Psychology as a Vocation
David G. Myers

There is one final lesson I have learned, which is that *psychology is a wonderful vocation.* Consider: What more fascinating subject could we study and teach than our own human workings? What teaching aims are more worthy than restraining intuition with critical thinking and judgmentalism with understanding? What subject is more influential in shaping values and lifestyles than our young science of psychology? [Dr. Myers continues in his correspondence by using a quotation to summarize his thoughts and feelings about choosing psychology as his career.]

There are "two sorts of jobs," wrote C. S. Lewis in *Screwtape Proposes a Toast* (1965):

> Of one sort, a [person] can truly say, "I am doing work which is worth doing. It would still be worth doing if nobody paid for it. But as I have no private means, and need to be fed and housed and clothed, I must be paid while I do it." The other kind of job is that in which people do work whose sole purpose is the earning of money: work which need not be, ought not to be, or would not be, done by anyone in the whole world unless it were paid.

I am thankful that I am blessed with a vocation that is decidedly in the first category. A vocation that is mind-expanding, full of fresh surprises, and focused on humanly significant questions.   ⟡

UCLA professor Steve Lopez, Ph.D., has expressed similar views about choosing psychology as his life's pursuit.

Exploring Meaningful Questions
Steven R. Lopez

I feel blessed for having chosen psychology as a profession. I have greatly appreciated the opportunity to carry out multiple roles as a teacher, clinician, and researcher. I have found each of these roles to be most rewarding. Oftentimes they complement each other; contributing to a very rich professional experience. But what I like most about being a psychologist is to think about and explore personally meaningful questions. For me questions concerning ethnicity, culture, and human behavior are of particular interest. What role does culture play in the lives of people? How should one integrate this knowledge in counseling or treating an individual or family?

Questions of ethnicity and culture, especially on a personal level, first grabbed my attention in college during the early 1970s. I was struggling with questions of ethnic identity. I knew I was of Mexican descent but was I Mexican American? Chicano? (a new word for me at the time), or a "Tio Taco"? (Uncle Tom) as it was rumored. Beginning my junior year I decided to learn more about my heritage through classes (e.g., Anthropology, Mexican literature), travel (semester abroad in Mexico), talks with key relatives, and long hours in the Arizona Historical Museum located in my home town of Tucson, Arizona. Although ethnic identity is a dynamic construct, tied closely to one's social and historical context, I figured out my ethnic niche, for the most part. I am Mexican American, Chicano, and Latino, but like any person who identifies with one of these labels, I have my own unique space within this ethnicity.

Psychology provided me a means to explore questions of identity and culture. Although I learned to frame my studies of ethnicity and culture in academic terms, the original passion was derived from very personal questions. Over the years, questions of ethnicity and culture have become less personal and more professional. For example, I have studied how mental health clinicians consider culture in their clinical work and how culture may be related to the way families cope with their relative's serious mental illness. However, underlying these more academic questions is a personal understanding of how culture and ethnicity contribute to who I am and what I do. I strongly believe that this personal understanding contributes greatly to my efforts to advance our knowledge of the relationship between culture and behavior and its implications for helping others.

As students explore their career options, I encourage them to pursue directions for which they have passion. By doing so, they will most likely enjoy what they do and, in turn, carry out their work at the highest possible level. Psychology provided me a way to pursue my passion. For that I am most grateful.

PSYCHOLOGY IN THE TWENTY-FIRST CENTURY

PSYCHOLOGISTS ARE FOUND IN ALL WALKS OF LIFE

Within today's fast-paced world, psychologists are viewed as innovators who have the theoretical, research, and interpersonal knowledge to incorporate new approaches from established backgrounds to meet the changing needs of people and societies. People from academic and clinical psychology programs are now in the United States Congress, work for the FBI, and advise the Department for Homeland Security. They also provide disaster relief during national emergencies, such as assisting with evacuated children following the aftermath of Hurricane Katrina. From a job perspective, advertisements for well-paid psychology positions have been posted at such vastly different places as the Security and Exchange Commission (SEC) and the Library of Congress.

And psychologists are varied in their career pursuits. Well-known private practitioner and past American Psychological Association (APA) president

Theodore Blau, Ph.D. (now deceased), used to consult to his local police department in Florida. Neil Wollman, Ph.D., continues to pursue research as a senior fellow of the Peace Studies Institute at Manchester College, Indiana. Likewise, renowned psychological mystery author Jonathan Kellerman, Ph.D., put his child clinical work aside to pursue his first love—writing. Psychologist Judith Rodin, Ph.D., put her innovative research in health-related issues aside to become president of the University of Pennsylvania, then president of the Rockefeller Foundation.

Reasons for Pursuing Psychology
Judith Rodin

I became a psychologist because I fell in love with the field through a dazzling introductory psych course my freshman year at Penn. I had intended on being a French major, but was captivated by the systematic study of human behavior. After all, what a gift it would be to make a career based on under-standing how people think and why they act as they do! Reflecting back over thirty-five years after that intro course, what a great decision I made.

During my scholarly career, I have chosen to study the interaction be-tween mind and body—how brain and behavior influence psychological outcomes; including health, illness, and even mortality. In this work, we studied obesity, eating disorders, stress and coping, and aging. I worked with extraordinary colleagues and students, as we helped to push the frontiers of new knowledge. It was exciting and enormously gratifying to be considered among the pioneers in the newly emerging fields of health psychology and behavioral medicine. These new fields were in the vanguard of so much of the important interdisciplinary work pushing the fields of psychology, biology, and medicine today.

One of the great joys of my career has been teaching gifted college stu-dents. Many times a year, I meet someone who took one of my courses and talks about how it impacted him or her. This is an extraordinary opportunity and one that continues to make me feel humble and grateful.

Good career choices also take unexpected turns, so the best planning in the world does not always predict what you do next. I became dean of the Graduate School and then provost at Yale University and then president of the University of Pennsylvania, the most satisfying job imaginable. And I believe my training as a psychologist was critical to my success in these roles!

My training in data analysis and comfort with empirical data made me a strong user of high-quality information for decision making. My training in inductive and deductive reasoning made me a highly effective strategic planner. And training in observing and understanding human behavior was an extremely useful leadership skill. Psychology has the breadth and depth to take you from the most theoretical to the most applied issues and, for me, has been wonderful preparation for life. As I embark on the next phase—to become president of the Rockefeller Foundation—I know once again how widely I will call upon my training and skills as a psychologist.

As you can see, the discipline of psychology is a tremendously varied field and produces many successful and talented individuals who have channeled their years of solid academic and experiential work into fulfilling and challenging pursuits across their life span. They teach, they consult, they help people. They conduct research and perform individual and group assessments, and they become advocates and administrators, as well as teachers, researchers, and authors.

Surely, the preparation toward a psychology degree brings with it not only the source of much creative knowledge, but also the key to many exciting life adventures. Even if you are not sure about a particular college major or a specific career path at this time (and as you will see by the many stories in this book, life pursuits take many unexpected twists), the skills learned through courses in psychology offer exciting possibilities and challenges. A true story by Ellen Berscheid, Ph.D., Regents Professor of Psychology at the University of Minnesota, demonstrates many of these points.

Life as a Psychologist: Reflections
Ellen S. Berscheid

I will always be grateful to psychology because it vanquished my enemy—boredom. Boredom was my personal "beast in the jungle" (to borrow from the title of Henry James's short story)—always lurking and ready to pounce, bringing its ugly companions, depression and lassitude, with it. In high school, for example, the classes were boring, the teachers were boring, and, being smart enough to get along easily academically (except in Beginning Typing, where I was given a D for chewing gum and having a "bad attitude"), I had plenty of time on my hands to stir up excitement among my fellow students who often looked to me for entertainment and to create trouble for the teachers.

Officially, I was viewed as a "disciplinary problem" (as the principal put it in one of his many telephone calls to my parents); in other words, a pain in the necks and posteriors of my teachers. I graduated early, eager to get on with whatever there was to get on with. My mother insisted on college. "Try it," she pleaded; "just one semester—you'll like it." With a sigh and to please my mother, I went. College wasn't as easy as high school and it wasn't as boring but, still, it wasn't all that interesting either, and I dropped out periodically, re-enrolling when whatever else I was doing became even more boring.

The last time I went back to college I saw a notice pinned to a bulletin board saying that the Psychology Department was offering a new seminar titled "Perception and Cognition." Although I nominally was an English major with vague thoughts of going on to law school, I impulsively signed up. I signed up because I thought it was going to be a seminar in extrasensory perception (ESP) and precognition and that I would learn the secrets of clairvoyance, mind-reading, and spoon-bending. By the time I realized my mistake, I was hooked on learning what was infinitely more interesting—how people perceive and think about other people.

I had so many questions—questions that no one could answer, for interpersonal perception and cognition was a new field within psychology at the time. At the end of the semester I had performed well enough that the professor asked if I would like a job as his research assistant—he had just received a grant to study interpersonal perception and cognition, investigating such questions as why people like and dislike the people they do. It was an honor to be asked because I was only an undergraduate and not a psychology major (as reflected in my original expectations for the course, which I wisely never shared with the professor), so I accepted and discovered that research was a way to answer all those questions I had. It was not only enjoyable, it was exciting!

My life in psychology started with that seminar. Indeed, I sometimes think my life itself started with that seminar, for I have never been bored since—not even for an instant, which seems a kind of miracle. Perhaps it is that there still are so many questions yet to be answered—important questions whose answers not only will be interesting in themselves but will someday improve the human condition.

My only regret is that I was born too soon, for right now is unquestionably the most exciting time for anyone to enter psychology and to become a research psychologist. For example, social neuroscience (how our brains process information about other people) is in its infancy. Affective neuroscience (how our emotions and feelings influence the processing of information) is also in its infancy. Affective neuroscience engages relationship science because it is people with whom we are in close relationship who most often generate the emotions and feelings we experience in our daily lives.

The study of interpersonal relationships is itself in its early childhood. Now is the time to begin at the beginning of the unraveling of some of the

most important mysteries psychology has ever tackled. How I envy those
who can take advantage of the opportunity!

A DISCIPLINE ON THE RISE

Psychology is certainly a discipline with a bright future. Among jobs requiring a college degree, it is expected to be one of the fastest-growing fields
in the United States through the next decade and is expected to keep growing
steadily. As noted, opportunities for work in psychology are expanding in
number and scope. For example, there is a noticeable increase in securing the
knowledge of psychologists in sports. Recently, a psychologist colleague of
mine, Valerie Lorenz, Ph.D., was asked to serve on a joint commission for the
National Collegiate Athletic Association (NCAA) to investigate the effects of
gambling on college sports. In addition, sports psychologists as a group often
consult to local professional teams to ensure their peak performance and to
assist the players' in adjusting to being away from family responsibilities during training camps. Given a solid background in the psychological
aspects of behavior, sports psychologists follow a career direction that truly
becomes a grand adventure rather than a chore to secure income.

PROTECTING THE COUNTRY

Another recent occurrence is the need for psychologists to share their
expertise in the protection of our country. To meet this need, the University
of Maryland established a new Homeland Security Center of Excellence,
which will span both international and domestic issues. Areas of work for
psychologists will include examining the sources of terrorism and responses
to it; analyzing the psychological impact of terrorism on society; and increasing the American public's preparedness, response, and resilience in the
face of threats. Psychological experts will be needed to examine the motivation and intent of terrorists in order to develop strategies and tools to
improve counteractions, such as understanding and forecasting the magni-
tude of the terrorist threat and formulating effective response strategies.

REPRESENTING THE PEOPLE

Further, there are now five congressional representatives on Capitol Hill
who have been instrumental in advocating for mental issues. For instance,

Tim Murphy, Ph.D., from southwestern Pennsylvania started the Mental Health Caucus, while Brian Baird, Ph.D., who represents Southwest Washington, is cofounder of the Congressional Caucus to Fight and Control Methamphetamine. Congressman Baird has also hosted a forum to educate members of Congress and their staffs about post-traumatic stress disorder (PTSD) and other psychological challenges faced by many armed service members returning from Iraq and Afghanistan.

Dianne Watson, Ed.D., of Los Angeles, like Congressman Murphy a member of the Mental Health Caucus, is a strong advocate to provide comprehensives services to victims of trafficking women and children, as well as expand care to armed services women and men who have been sexually assaulted. Likewise, Tom Osborne, Ph.D., of Lincoln, Nebraska, gained attention for legislating a comprehensive strategy to address suicide prevention and behavioral health problems in high school and colleges. Additionally, Ted Strickland, Ph.D., of Ohio (who was the first psychologist to be elected to Congress over a decade ago) has been the moving force to have federal funds allocated to create mental health courts throughout the United States.

HEALTH PSYCHOLOGY

Psychology is also at the forefront of illness prevention, rather than focusing merely on the diagnosing and treating of disorders. Psychologists strive to help people learn how to make healthy behavior a routine part of everyday living. For example, the subdiscipline of health psychology clearly plays a very important role not only in conducting research that identifies linkages between particular behaviors and health outcomes but also in arranging interventions that can significantly contribute to the health of whole communities. Indeed, many difficulties facing society today are problems about behavior: for instance, drug addiction, poor interpersonal relationships, violence at home, in the schools, and in the street, and the potential harm we do to our environment. Psychologists are at the forefront in contributing solutions to these problems because of their extensive training in collecting and analyzing data, as well as in developing intervention strategies—in other words, by applying scientific principles to the difficulties that face our everyday environments.

EXPANDING PSYCHOLOGY'S SCOPE

Further, an aging world points to the need for more research and practice in adapting homes and workplaces for older people to make their lives productive and meaningful. With this focus in mind, psychology professor Tom Prohaska, Ph.D., and his colleagues in the Department of Public Health at the University of Illinois, Chicago, have developed innovative community programs for older adults with perspectives that stemmed from basic and applied research that have paved the way for public policy. Likewise, the ever-increasing number of women in the workplace calls for employers to accommodate the needs of families and for psychologists to apply their knowledge of child development and family functioning to workplace productivity. As these examples demonstrate, psychologists continue to be instrumental in helping organizations and employers make the important and effective changes that are needed for the inclusion of all people.

Research advances in learning and memory, and the integration of physical and mental health care, also make becoming a psychologist more exciting now than ever. Psychology covers both information processing and the study of normal and abnormal functioning. Whereas one subdiscipline promotes positive health habits through preventative counseling programs designed to help people achieve goals such as smoking reduction or weight loss, in another neuropsychologists study the relationship between the brain and behavior and then perform extensive testing to determine accommodations for disorders or to plan rehabilitation after trauma or accidents. As continued research and clinical work yield new information, these findings build upon the ongoing body of knowledge that practitioners rely on in their everyday work with clients and patients. Norman Abeles, Ph.D., former APA President, and Director of the Clinical Neuropsychological Laboratory and Memory Assessment Center at Michigan State University, explores psychology's changing face in the next section.

___

Psychology in Today's World
Norman Abeles

Psychology in the twenty-first century is somewhat different then it was in the last century—at least it is different than it was thirty to forty years ago. Then the major applied areas were clinical psychology, counseling psychology, school psychology, and industrial/organizational psychology. Today, in addition to those areas there are lots of newer applied areas and subareas such as health psychology, sports psychology, family psychology, rehabilitation psychology, neuropsychology, clinical geropsychology, pain management, and psychopharmacology, just to name a few of the more widely known applied areas.

I became interested in the area of aging about twenty years ago. Not only was I getting older, but some of our clinical psychology graduate students were interested in life span developmental topics, and aging is clearly within that area. Many of these students had grandparents who were beginning to complain about memory problems, and indeed some of those grandparents had developed Alzheimer's disease or similar disorders.

In order to further study aging issues we developed a research strategy plan to study memory complaints in older adults. This included recruiting community dwelling older adults to participate in mood and memory workshops. Lots of people volunteered to participate, and most of these people had responded to our ad, which inquired if they were worried about their memory and were willing to participate in workshops.

We met with small groups of these people for seven weeks for one and one-half hour sessions each week. We first checked to see if they were depressed and/or anxious, and then we checked on the extent of their memory complaints and worked only with people who had no serious objective memory problems compared to other normal older adults. Of course, the participants often told us that their memory was much better when they were younger and perhaps that is why they were worried about their memory.

After seven weeks we tested these participants again and found that their memory complaints were significantly reduced and their memory complaints were more a function of being mildly or moderately depressed or anxious. So as we helped them talk about their worries and anxieties and gave them some instructions about memory techniques, their memory complaints tended to diminish.

It should be noted that these workshops did not improve memory functions, but they did show improvement in memory complaints. You may ask why we should even be concerned with people who just complain about their memory but actually have little or no objective memory problems. Several answers are given to that concern. First, it is possible that some people with memory complaints do develop more serious memory problems, so that mood and memory checkups are helpful from a preventive point of view. Second, we certainly encourage people to get checkups for vision and hearing, and sometimes these checkups require relatively minor adjustments. We certainly do not want to wait until one is close to being deaf or blind before intervening.

Third, since memory complaints are often a sign of depression and/or anxiety, early checkups and treatments can help to reduce anxiety and worry and prevent more serious concerns from developing. So that is where we began. We moved from there to investigate the relationship between attention and memory, the relationship between anxiety and depression, and the overall issues of quality of life, end-of-life decisions, mental health care for adults, and ethical issues involved in working with older adults.

In the meantime I was elected president of the 150,000-member American Psychological Association in 1997 and helped to establish an office on aging within that association! While I served as president we also developed guidelines in the assessment of cognitive disorders and other dementias. In addition, one of my task forces developed a helpful brochure on "What the Practitioner Needs to Know in Working with Older Adults."

I also attended the White House Conference on Aging, which is held every ten years, and presented papers at professional and scientific meetings and trained a lot of graduate students to work with older adults and to do research on a range of problems of older adults. Our grad students get a vast amount of training in geropsychology (older adults) and neuropsychology (brain behavior relationships), and they have to know something about pharmacology because older adults tend to take numerous medications and one has to know how those affect the person. So, with a startup interest in older adults, I have tried to trace very quickly a broader base of practice and research that may be of interest to many of you.

PSYCHOLOGICAL COLLABORATION IN EVERYDAY PRACTICE

Although many psychologists work independently on their research or in private clinical practice or consulting, they frequently collaborate with other professionals. You may find them working side by side with other scientists, physicians, lawyers, school personnel, computer experts, and engineers to design better and more efficient methods to solve daily problems. For example, Robert Hamm, Ph.D., from Virginia Commonwealth University works within a medical school animal lab with neurologists and other medical researchers to better understand the consequences of head injuries. Alan H. Kawamoto, Ph.D., at the University of California at Santa Cruz shares ideas with other cognitive scientists to understand how information is presented and processed, using computer simulations and empirical methods to explore the areas of parallel distributed processing, and in doing so attempt to answer the lifelong question, "Why do people feel, think, and act the way they do?" Within a more personal and interpersonal sphere, private practice clinical psychologist and sex therapist Bruce Friedin, Ph.D., from Long Island, New York, has collaborated with family practitioners and other physicians who specialize in the sexual dysfunctions of men and women, marital infidelity, sexual trauma, and child abuse, as well as healthy sexual relationships in marriage.

Another psychologist, Stephen Fabick, Ph.D., has been able to collaborate with a variety of professional colleagues through his activities as president of Psychologists for Social Responsibility, an international organization that uses psychological knowledge and skills to promote justice and peace at community, national, and international levels. One of his manuals, *US & THEM: The Challenge of Diversity*, was selected as one of the top U.S. programs promoting racial and ethnic dialogue. As a clinical and consulting psychologist in Birmingham, Michigan, he has had many opportunities to speak about conflict resolution and reducing the risk of terrorism. In viewing his career, he spoke of the following critical times that influence his daily activities.

Social Responsibility
Stephen D. Fabick

One of the rewarding aspects of my career as a psychologist has been the opportunity to apply psychological theory and my clinical skills in my peace psychology work. I went into psychology as most of us do, with conscious and unconscious needs to resolve my personal conflicts (within myself and my family) as well as to have some broader impact upon injustices and conflicts in society. That motivation continued unabated, but I had to guard against overdoing it too, i.e., pace myself so I don't burn out. I try to maintain a balance between my pro bono work and business, as well as some synthesis of them so I feel less fragmented, e.g., doing conflict resolution work with groups on a pro bono basis through Psychologists for Social Responsibility (PsySR) in Michigan and with our national organization, but also conflict resolution work with individual intrapsychic conflicts, marital therapy for couple's conflicts, and family therapy for problems in families, and finally conflict resolution work in organizations as part of my consulting work.

I've found that my work with PsySR and also with the Society for the Study of Peace, Conflict and War (Division 48 of the American Psychological Association) provides me with a sense of shared vision and support as well as friendships with people I greatly admire. Doing this kind of work in such collegial networks makes reading the front page less depressing than it did twenty-five years ago before I became involved with these groups.

I'm less prone to "compassion fatigue" when I feel that we are at least "lighting a candle."

Of course, many psychologists teach at colleges and universities and find it quite rewarding. For instance, John Harvey, Ph.D., an esteemed professor of social psychology at the University of Iowa, has conducted research for over thirty-five years but relishes working with students.

Memorable Moments in the Classroom
John Harvey

The activities I have treasured most in being a college teacher for over thirty years are seeing many students develop their lives in quite positive ways, hearing about their lives and families for years after they graduate, and sometimes being of assistance (e.g., writing letters of reference for them) for years into the future.

I was trained as a social psychologist. For years, I studied how people change attitudes and make attributions about others' behavior. In the last decade, I have begun teaching two courses that have special relevance to our lives. One is Close Relationships. Obviously, students love to analyze close relationships and why they form, sometimes continue, and sometimes end. This course hopefully helps them deal with the great flux they see in the world of relationships (including sometimes divorce in their family).

The other course is a large class on Loss and Trauma. In this course, I hear about many personal and family tragedies. It also is uplifting to see students have the courage to be open about their losses and to work diligently to make something positive in the context of the losses. Many students have come back to the class to tell stories of how they coped with loss (e.g., sometimes the loss of a parent, or a significant other in a car accident). Their courage and attempt to find meaning in their loss represent a major life lesson for all the other students who hear their story.

CAREERS PATHS WITHIN PSYCHOLOGY

Careers directions within the field of psychology are shaped by level of education, career interests, living preferences, and commitment to family concerns. Persons who obtain master's and doctoral degrees in psychology will usually have more opportunities in their career development within the field. For example, they can obtain community college teaching positions or conduct research and teach in most four-year colleges, or they can be principal investigators in research labs and in receiving research grants. They also can provide a myriad of clinical psychological services and be reimbursed through insurers. Although many intellectually stimulating and financially rewarding jobs are available to psychology graduates (B.A. level), those individuals who complete postgraduate work often find a richer and more diverse lifestyle within the practice of psychology itself. As noted, professional psychologists are employed in the government, within industry, and in private practices dealing with the application, research, and teaching of psychology principles.

This breadth of interests is well represented by mentioning one group of students who received bachelor's degrees in psychology and obtained admission to various graduate programs to pursue master's and doctoral degrees. Besides attending programs inside the discipline of psychology (including specializations in organizational, school, social, and developmental psychology), these particular students went to medical and law schools in addition to completing graduate programs in social work, genetic counseling, kinesiology, biophysics, theology, and speech pathology. Thus, there are many paths to one's life work, but as you can see the study of psychology is both varied and detailed enough to pursue many career options. This next story by Ellen Lent, Ph.D., provides glimpses into the capricious nature of career development.

Consulting as a Psychologist
Ellen Lent

In my twelfth-grade year, a VISTA (Volunteers in Service to America) representative spoke at my high school, and I was convinced this was my postsecondary career choice. My parents did not agree, however, and in April of my senior year they required me to apply to two local women's colleges. I was accepted at both and decided on the one that offered more financial aid. When I enrolled, I stated my intention to major in psychology. However, my chosen college lacked a psychology department. I drifted along until junior year, when I finally declared as an English major. My work-study job was helping students in the office of the dean and registrar. After college, I worked as a university admissions officer for graduate programs.

When I moved and began to look for a new job, I approached the local university counseling center, since I felt very capable of working with students. The director advised me to look into college student personnel graduate programs, especially at Ohio State University. Five years later, after a good deal of graduate work in comparative literature, I found myself entering the master's program in student personnel at Ohio State, with a minor in counseling psychology.

More work in university admissions and student life followed. I took the LSAT and applied to one law school, unsuccessfully. Later, as an assistant dean, I decided I needed a Ph.D. to progress to more interesting positions. With an acceptance to the English doctoral program at University of Minnesota in hand, I approached the campus career center for a job to pay my expenses. After about ten minutes, my interviewer said, "Ellen, you don't need a doctorate in English. You should go into training and development. There are lots of corporations around here who like people with weird backgrounds like yours!"

I had three months before school started, so I began researching training and development. What I learned was very appealing. I accepted a contractual position in human resources research at Control Data Corporation, asked for a year's extension at University of Minnesota, and let September pass by. I was working alongside a number of Ph.D. graduates in counseling and organizational psychology and finding the work very fulfilling. I was offered a permanent position in training and development, expanded to career planning and executive coaching, and had a very enjoyable career within the company for five years. By that time I was ready to return to school and learn more about career decision making and job satisfaction. So I took a statistics course, studied for the GREs, applied to eight programs, and was accepted at seven of them. My very supportive husband, a psychology Ph.D. himself, obtained a job offer and we moved to Michigan State University. I decided to major in counseling psychology, since I wanted a psychology license, and I focused on vocational and organizational issues because of my previous work experience.

Back to the career center interview: If I hadn't met that very perspicacious lady that day, I'd probably be an underutilized English Ph.D. by now. What's the connection, though? I believe that I chose English because analyzing fiction is the next-best thing to studying human behavior. But I'm all for career counseling at the college level (since I didn't get any), so I'm now consulting to a company that is developing a web-enabled site for career exploration at the high school and college level! I wonder what might have been if I had started out in psychology? I'll never know, but I have always trusted the serendipity factor in career planning.

Along your life's journey, you will define yourself in many ways depending on your age, focus, and responsibilities. Success means sticking to a broad path and realizing that your primary career choice may have many branches that are all quite good (win-win situations). But it takes exposure and to these varying branches experience to realize the possibilities and the goodness of fit to your desired lifestyle.

So, look through this book; also read articles from journals and magazines by psychologists who have made a difference and who are doing the type of work that you can visualize yourself doing. Find out what has been exciting and meaningful to them, and then decide which path to consider. Don't be afraid to e-mail or talk to these people—they are human and approachable. At least go to their university or other work-related websites for information about them. Also, talk to your teachers and professors; they do want to help and because of their knowledge and experiences have something very important to offer you.

Gain experience where you can, through paid or volunteer work. Go to seminars and to conventions, even if these are supposed to be for professional psychologists. There is no better place to see the variety of career possibilities than at a national or regional convention within a particular discipline. You gain incredible exposure and an awareness of what the field is all about. You also hear major contributors within the field. Discovering your life's pursuit, something that you really want and love, is exceedingly important, especially in the context of extending yourself within your family and community.

Also, gain mentors along the way. Become assistants, whether in teaching, research, or direct therapeutic support. This is an excellent way to discover your personal strengths and weakness and to visualize yourself doing this work daily. Take as many practicum positions and internships as possible; and if you have the time, complete postdoctoral and other training leading to specialized certification within a personal and professional interest.

And travel. In striving to create an ideal picture of your future self, be aware of possible employment and lifestyle settings. Do you enjoy the outdoors or city activities? Does your profession offer more job opportunities in small towns, where you may have more responsibilities at a younger age, than in large cities that may be saturated with many specialists, but with more job openings, more people, and so on? Also, what type of atmosphere do you prefer: campus life, a small office setting, or corporate structures? Consider these alternatives as you thoroughly research and discuss your future as a psychologist.

CHAPTER 2

Psychology as the "Right" Career Choice

STRIVING TO FULFILL YOUR NEEDS

As a broad and exciting subject of study, psychology has many advantages over other disciplines. In one sense, it is an opportunity to study yourself in depth, while at the same time viewing how you relate to the outer world—something that you probably already attempt to do on a daily basis! However, it is also a behavioral science that offers you the skills to become an independent researcher, scholar, and clinician, and provides challenging opportunities to improve lives. Few other areas of study can claim such a feat and prepare students for the next phase in their careers, no matter what the path.

As you read the next chapter of this book, you will quickly discover that this path is never straight, and often presents many curves and just "dumb luck," as one later professor suggests. The seasoned professionals in this book will not only offer you glimpses of their careers, but will also address the twists and turns that confronted them and the many choices they made based on personal interest while balancing their personal needs. Oftentimes, you are bound to quickly discover that you just do not have all the answers, although for a time you actually thought you did.

As you will hear from these next illustrious psychologists, you need not get discouraged. They have made careers out of their curiosity about themselves, their successes and failures, and by sheer happenstance. In striving to be true to their own desires and to make differences in other people's lives, they overcame rejection and barriers to become highly accomplished researchers, theorists, teachers, and clinicians. For Robert Sternberg, Ph.D., IBM Professor of Psychology and Education at Yale University, the study of psychology offered him the "right" platform to truly understand himself and, in turn, to contribute his findings to the larger world. By comparison, for Marilyn Erickson, Ph.D., who is now professor emerita from Virginia Commonwealth University, the study of psychology was just an extension of her childhood interests, experiences, and intellectual pursuits. Her career as an expert in childhood psychopathology placed her at the forefront in guiding the child clinical field and offered her the opportunity to mentor many generations of students in their quest of knowledge and practice.

Understanding Yourself
Robert J. Sternberg

I study psychology to understand the problems that have arisen in my own life. I started off with the study of intelligence because I did poorly on IQ tests as a child. I wanted to understand why. I eventually came to the conclusion that intelligence comprises three aspects: analytical, creative, and practical. The analytical aspect is what is measured by conventional tests, including the SAT and the ACT. The creative and practical aspects are largely unmeasured by these tests. Our research suggests that the three aspects of intelligence are, in large degree, independent. So someone could be, say, high in the analytical (academic) aspect of intelligence, but not particularly high in the practical aspect, or vice versa. Our research also suggests that the creative and practical aspects of intelligence are at least as important for success in life as the analytical one, and probably more so.

A second problem I have studied is love. I started studying love at a time in my life when my own love life was not going so well. I eventually devised a theory of love according to which love comprises three main elements: intimacy, passion, and commitment. Intimacy is one's feelings of closeness, trust, connectedness, and caring. Passion is one's feelings of intense longing and desire for someone. Commitment is one's feeling of irrevocable dedication to a relationship. Diffferent kinds of love emerge from different combinations of the three elements.

In sum, psychology is a great way to understand and even work out one's own problems. And that is what it has been for me.

Directional Changes, Mentors, and Passions
Marilyn T. Erickson

I never had to wonder what I was going to do "when I grew up" because I always knew I wanted to study children's behavior; most of my jobs as a teenager involved children (i.e., babysitter, inner-city pool lifeguard, playground instructor).

The process of becoming a psychologist, however, didn't always go smoothly. As a sophomore transfer student to Brown University, I was told that my record wasn't good enough to be a psychology major; so when an English professor invited me to become an honors student in English, I accepted with enthusiasm. In retrospect, the decision was probably a good one because the honors program required writing a paper (and getting plenty of feedback) every week for two years.

I quickly realized that I was still primarily interested in studying behavior and approached the Psychology Department chairman to find out what I needed to do to go to graduate school in psychology. He replied that if I took courses in statistics and experimental psychology and did well in them, he would admit me to the graduate program at Brown. I think he was gambling on the notion that these courses would greatly discourage this English major. But I did well (even loved statistics), and he honored his promise. As I participated in the Brown seminars, I was sure that I was the worst student ever to set foot there; everyone knew more psychology than I.

Then a wonderful event occurred. Brown hired Lew Lipsitt as a new faculty member, and Lew accepted me for thesis research. Saved by the perfect mentor! Just as things were going well, my husband announced that he had a chance to get into one of the best postdoctoral programs in his field. With a master's in hand and three weeks before classes were starting, we drove to the University of Washington in Seattle. Not having had time to apply for the doctoral program, all I could do was to beg the chairman to admit me as a special student. After one quarter, I was admitted and given assistantships until I finished the program less than two years later. Like Brown, Washington had many stimulating professors and competent graduate students. My interests in experimental, developmental, and clinical child psychology were perfectly compatible with the movement in applied behavior analysis with children begun by Bijou, Baer, Lovaas, and Birnbrauer; fellow students included Todd Risley and Bob Wahler.

While I was studying for prelims, my husband went on interviews for academic positions in physiological psychology and received many offers. We decided that Duke University would be a great place to begin his career, and both of us assumed that, with three universities within commuting distance and many job openings, I would have no trouble finding an academic position. What no one had told me was that many universities were not hiring women in tenure track positions, and I hadn't even noticed that none of my professors were women. I did, however, receive an offer from the University of North Carolina–Chapel Hill Psychiatry Department—they needed someone who could help a small group of psychiatrists with a research project and who had some skills in testing preschool children for the pediatrics clinic.

While it is true that I had research skills, in graduate school I was led to believe that I would be doing my own research; in addition, my experience with preschool testing was obtained primarily from working as a research assistant. The many challenges I faced as a new Ph.D. became great assets in subsequent professional settings. I learned how to use clinical settings to produce publishable research. Because my research activities were not of interest to my psychology colleagues, I learned early how to function as an independent researcher. I was also eased into teaching by first supervising graduate students and residents individually, then teaching small groups in seminars, and finally teaching larger groups of students.

Six months after beginning to work with medical students and residents in pediatrics, I was asked to join a small interdisciplinary training group. Within less than ten years, that group of four became a faculty of over forty people from fourteen disciplines with both state and federal funding. Within a few years of being tenured, I had administrative responsibility for six psychologists and served as the research consultant for the interdisciplinary faculty.

Almost nothing during my ten years at Chapel Hill was easy, but the challenges provided opportunities to develop new skills that continued to serve me well in the subsequent thirty years as a faculty member in two psychology departments.

COLLEGE AND CAREER GOALS

You will be a more successful student if you think seriously about directional possibilities when applying to colleges and planning for majors and specific careers. Knowing why you are in school helps you see the relevance between what you are doing now and how this will serve you later, either on the job or in graduate school. Seeing these connections may enhance your motivation. You can visualize important payoffs if you develop clear educational and career goals early in your college experience. For instance, planning gives you extra time to identify the courses relevant to your future and to volunteer for extracurricular activities that will enable you to develop useful skills.

Even if you don't have all the answers, don't get discouraged. You may simply need more information before you know what you want. And that is what this book is all about! Reading the memoirs and reflections provided here will give you much "food for thought" in making those tough choices. Also, listening to the "voices" of the psychologists who have contributed their stories will show you the many twists and turns careers may take. Even if you know which courses to take and have planned extracurricular experiences to help you develop the knowledge and skills you'll need for later success, you may take comfort in these career reflections, realizing that many paths lie ahead and that you can accomplish much by being open to all possibilities. Fortunately, the discipline of psychology offers many paths for the interested adventurer, as clinical psychologist Bill Levin, Ph.D., shares in the next story.

Why Didn't I Go into Another Field?

Bill Levin

I considered four other fields before I decided on psychology as my main pursuit. In high school, I thought I would want to become a dentist like my father. However, working in his office on Saturdays for a while convinced me otherwise. I liked developing x-rays for him, and hearing patients call him "Dr. Levin" was appealing. The thought of having my hands in mouths all day, however, was a real turn off!

Next in college, I expected to become a physician. Although I studied very hard, I fared poorly in the traditional sciences but was very successful in nonscientific courses. Since I went to a very competitive college and had a limited science background, I retook some science courses, doing pretty well in summer school. Eventually, I faced the reality that I wouldn't get the needed recommendation from my college committee and chose psychology instead.

Had I become a physician, I would most likely have become a pediatrician or a psychiatrist. In retrospect, I am relieved that I didn't become a physician. The changes in that profession have rendered medicine a less than desirable field now. Also, for a short while I considered becoming a rabbi, probably because that is what my roommate eventually became. I even gave one sermon at a Friday night service. Temperamentally, though, I wasn't a good match for the rabbinate at that time. It also surprises me that I never considered law as a career. I have the requisite skills and interest and always loved history and have been increasingly intrigued by politics as an observer. In short, however, I ended up in psychology because the courses fascinated me, I wanted to figure myself out, and I had an abiding interest in helping others, and the idea of being called "Doctor"—having a substantial professional career like my parents—felt good to me.

Over time, my therapeutic style has become increasingly spiritually oriented in a supportive manner. The privileged opportunity to get to know people so well, to bear witness and validate the importance of their life stories, to help so many people, to be fascinated by life and its manifestation in all of us, and to learn from others from so many different backgrounds—the possibilities of getting close to others' core experiences, to be magnanimous in the process, to teach clients how to ride the waves of feeling and time, making peace with our fears, to facilitate the reconstruction of lives as meaningful, fun, and satisfying—to me, this is fabulous!

PSYCHOLOGY: AN EVER-CHANGING DISCIPLINE

Psychology is a science of much exploration and dynamic change. Not only are there new areas to study and apply this knowledge, but new career opportunities continue to appear. Today's graduates face a myriad of everyday societal problems such as job loss, alienation, sexually related diseases, school violence, drug abuse, and anxiety and depression-related symptoms; consequently, many psychology programs involve more counseling and more developmental theory courses than ever before. Courses such as psychology of sexuality, psychology of aging, and psychology of sports focus attention on current events and their impact on life stages and life events. Each topic presages fieldwork possibilities for the career-minded psychology graduate.

The trend toward helping human behavior is evident in psychology curriculums that now offer more courses in clinical and developmental areas than in the heretofore prominent areas of experimental psychology and industrial and organizational psychology. Psychology is increasingly engaged in service work to alleviate human suffering, and courses in family dynamics, criminality, and the psychology of women suggest that few areas remain remote from scrutiny. Counseling psychologist Joan Offerle, Ph.D., shares her search for a caretaking career that would include an interesting and balanced lifestyle.

Transitions from Graduate School to Practice
Joan Offerle

I chose psychology instead of cultural anthropology for two reasons. One is that I thought I could best deal with people one at a time in terms of understanding them. Second, while I love to travel, I thought I would want a home and permanency of location; it seemed that as an anthropologist, I would have to locate to various cultures over the course of a career, and I didn't/don't want to move so much.

Upon receiving my doctorate degree from Virginia Commonwealth University, I expected that I would get post-doc supervision toward my licensure through a college counseling center job. When none was available when I relocated to Texas to be closer to my family, I was able to find a private practitioner who gladly supervised me, and by the time I had completed my required year of supervision, I had a pretty good grasp of how I wanted to run a practice of my own. So with a few carry-over clients, I launched a practice, and found some fill-in work. I did contract therapy at a grassroots-formed counseling center for gays and lesbians: my interest and workshops in grieving prepped me to work with HIV clients and I was comfortable with gay issues. A friend on faculty at the University of Texas asked if we could take a practicum student at that center, so I launched a practicum-training site and did all the supervision of psychology students from 1988–89 until May 2004. Turns out I loved supervising one to three students per year.

Another friend connected me with Southwest Texas University nearby: a member of the faculty who became seriously ill in the third week of the semester needed someone to take over two sections of a Marriage and Family course for the remainder of the semester. I did so, and somewhat enjoyed the undergraduate classes, but didn't care much for grading and commuting. The income it provided, though, was a great help in the first year of practice! More recently, I taught a course in Crisis Management at local St. Edwards University. Less commuting, but I found I really disliked teaching the graduate course, largely because there were such strictures about performance expectations for students, and because several of them were really unpleasant when they only earned "B's"! More verification, too, that I do my best work with individuals and couples or small groups.

Looking back, however, a turning point in my career occurred when I led a group for Survivors of Childhood Abuses at the YWCA in 1987. It was a good practice-builder, which is part of why I had led other groups for the Y and taught short-term skills courses (social, assertiveness) in the community schools for adults. In this case, it brought me my first dissociative client, who had survived familial and satanic cult abuse. In fact, of the ten women in the group at the Y, half of them came to me for individual therapy in the next few years. But the first one was the beginning of my specialization in multiple personality/dissociative identity disorders. This client was and remains a remarkable woman who taught me how to help her, while I helped her learn to trust and heal from her horrible mistreatment as a child.

At that time, neither I nor any of my colleagues had encountered MPD (multiple personality disorder) and cult abuse survivors; so while I dealt with my own shock by talking with all who would listen, I discovered someone who had been seeing such cases and was interested in forming a study group. Thank goodness! A handful of us joined together, read voraciously all that this experienced clinician had found in the literature, and shared case material. I was reassured that nationally respected therapists had blazed a trail in this arena, and began attending conferences and workshops on child abuse, cults, dissociation, and hypnotherapy. And I am pleased to report that I have been privileged to support the journey to wholeness of about a dozen clients over the last eighteen years.

Since I am single and childfree, working intensively with dissociative-disordered clients has been feasible in terms of my private life—I don't have conflicting demands from family and career. From the beginning, I set up a four-day workweek and typically scheduled clients from 10 A.M. to 6 P.M. This lets me enjoy my morning coffee, walking, reading. I take a 1 P.M. to 2 P.M. lunch hour, sometimes longer, either solo or with colleagues and friends. I share my suite with two licensed professional counselors, which is both cost effective and pleasant, and I am very happy with my present arrangements.

I went into psychology in part because I wanted a career that I could continue as long as I wanted—I don't see myself retiring until seventy or later, and even then might do a part-time practice. My clients may moan when I take my three- to five-week vacations, but they manage, and come back on schedule when I return. I've been able to spend three weeks in Brazil, a month in Ecuador, three weeks in Spain, five weeks in China, Tibet, and Nepal, and shorter times in Peru and some U.S. destinations.

All in all, I am happy in my career and my life. I love psychology—the questions keep being so interesting! And I do feel truly honored that people seek therapy with me, and that I am able to make a difference with many of them.

The following story is by Julian Rappaport, Ph.D., professor emeritus, University of Illinois, Urbana-Champaign. Dr. Rappaport was a pioneer in conceptualizing the field of community psychology in 1977. Here, he discusses how he found many satisfying paths within psychology through his research on such diverse topics as social policy, juvenile justice, self and mutual help support, social change, and the education of poor and minority children. He explains many of his choices in the following story of his career path.

Finding Meaning in Community Psychology
Julian Rappaport

I grew up in the 1950s and started college in the 1960s. At first I was not a very good student. I felt fortunate to even get into college. When I started college, I wanted to be a history teacher. When I started graduate school, I wanted to be a psychotherapist. I turned out to be neither. I never would have guessed that I would become a college professor who likes to write. That is something I learned to do over a long period of time. What I discovered, and what I tell my own students, is that the best way to learn is to explore topics that are of interest to you, rather than those you think you are supposed to be interested in, in order to gain success or acceptance. The best work you do will be on topics you care about.

Sometimes people advise high school and beginning college students to stay focused. That is good advice if you already know exactly what you want to do; but it is not such good advice if you want to explore. Psychology is a good field for exploration. The range of things psychologists do is so wide that it is possible to be both focused (on psychology) and flexible by realizing that the discipline ranges from people like me, who study social change, to people who study cognitive and biological processes (and everything in between). In my case, I found that as a community psychologist (who was trained as a clinical psychologist) I have been able to do my work in places that interest me.

I have conducted research with seriously disturbed mental patients; adolescents in trouble with the law; children in elementary schools; and ordinary citizens in church communities, self-help organizations, and universities. I have been able to pay attention to issues such as social justice, race relations, and citizen empowerment. Psychology is a discipline that lets us study people, organizations, and communities. We can even be concerned with how governments form social policy, make legal decisions, and distribute resources. For someone like me, who gets bored easily, being a psychologist has allowed me to be an explorer. Doing this with college and graduate students has also allowed me to stay connected with how the world is changing for young people. This is a career that has often made me feel like I am getting paid to have fun.

                                                                          ~

MAKING PSYCHOLOGY YOUR CAREER

Because the study of psychology is broadly based, almost any individual will find a keen interest in any number of its subdisciplines. There are programs and subject areas that focus on infant development, adolescence and youth, and gerontology. Applied research may focus on health and mental health intervention and research or rehabilitation after injury. Behavioral neuroscience and genetics are also a keen highlight of many programs, as are advances in artificial intelligence.

Clinical work, which remains the chief attraction to many who enter the field, offers coursework and experience in personality assessment, therapeutic intervention, crisis intervention, and group and family counseling. For those more interested in animal learning, such renowned centers as the Yerkes Laboratory in Atlanta, where speech patterns in monkeys are examined, have psychologists on staff to train or condition animals and to perform statistical analyses. Applied research is also the hallmark of multiple research and university centers that employ psychologists to coordinate studies with the National Institutes of Health (NIH) and Mental Health (NIMH) on such topics as depression, anxiety, or attention-deficit/hyperactivity disorder (ADHD). In brief, psychology as a discipline offers a vast richness to the understanding of animals, people, and the world in which we live and share with other people and other cultures. When you're a psychologist, your education never ends.

HIGH SCHOOL PREPARATION

As for many careers, a strong college preparatory high school education is a good beginning to continue in psychology-related paths. Although standard courses in English, history, social studies, and a foreign language remain important, science and math are crucial to provide the necessary skills for research and analysis in college psychology courses. Fortunately, many high schools offer courses in psychology that provide glimpses of what the field has to offer. Besides doing coursework, even during high school you should volunteer at settings that employ psychologists so you can see their daily work. People interested in psychology as a career should explore newspapers and magazines to discover interests in this broad field of study that offers many opportunities in a wide range of settings.

For example, the following ads appeared during the last year in a regularly published newspaper for psychologists entitled *The National Psychologist*. As you read through these ads, you will see some possibilities that exist within the discipline of psychology and begin to understand the various qualifications needed to apply for such positions. Don't be immediately discouraged by the high level of training needed to undertake these positions; rather, use them as a measuring stick in your life's quest.

> Licensed doctoral level psychologists needed throughout the U.S. to conduct (pre) employment, clinical interviews.
>
> Psychologist: (licensed) needed part-time for assessment, treatment, and behavioral medicine services with nursing home residents.
>
> Therapists with high professional ethics and clinical skills needed to provide counseling and consultation to day care centers and elementary schools.
>
> Counselor/Educator to assist in curriculum development and to teach graduate courses in a master's program in mental health counseling.
>
> Successful candidate to provide leadership for a post-doctoral master's program in clinical psychopharmacology, and to teach courses in biofeedback and neuropsychology.

THE UNDERGRADUATE YEARS

Whether actually having gone on to careers in psychology or moved into other fields, psychology majors cite courses in the principles of human behavior as especially important to life after college. From these courses they have gained insight into what motivates people to perform at their peak, which helps them whether as parents at home, managers on the job, or professionals in other fields. Many students credit their college psychology courses with teaching them how people, including themselves, learn. Above all, it is the rigorous training in the scientific method—the need to conduct thorough, objective research; analyze data logically; and put forth the findings with clarity—that gives psychology majors a competitive advantage in the workforce as they pursue their future careers.

BACHELOR'S DEGREE

A bachelor's degree in psychology qualifies a person to assist licensed psychologists and other professionals in community mental health centers, vocation rehabilitation offices, residential treatment centers, and correctional programs. Individuals with psychological training can also work as research or administrative assistants and are found employed as trainees in business and government. Within the federal government, candidates having at least twenty-four semester hours in psychology and at least one course in statistics qualify for entry-level positions.

Most undergraduate programs require a blend of science and liberal arts courses for a bachelor's degree in psychology. The courses usually include introductory psychology, experimental psychology, and statistics. Other required courses can be in learning, personality, abnormal psychology, social psychology, developmental psychology, physiological or comparative psychology, history and systems, and tests and measurement. Typically, you will be ready to take electives in psychology by the time you are a college junior. It is a good time to make graduate school plans so you can make wise choices about future courses and extracurricular activities during the last two years of college. Understand, however, that as long as you've taken some electives in psychology, you don't always need to have a bachelor's in psychology to get into a graduate program in the field.

POSTGRADUATE STUDY

Persons with a master's degree in psychology may work as industrial-organizational psychologists, find themselves employed in employee assistance programs (EAPs) or in human resources management, or they may work in schools as counselors or school psychologists. They may also work as psychological assistants in research labs or conduct psychological evaluations under the supervision of doctoral-level psychologists. A master's degree in psychology requires at least two years of full-time graduate study. Requirements usually include practical experience in an applied setting and a master's thesis based on an original research project. Competition for admission to graduate programs is keen. Some universities require applicants to have an undergraduate major in psychology. Others prefer only coursework in basic psychology with courses in the biological, physical, and social sciences; and statistics and mathematics.

A doctoral degree is usually required for employment as an independent licensed clinical or counseling psychologist. Psychologists with a doctor of philosophy (Ph.D.), the traditional program in psychology, qualify for a wide range of teaching, research, clinical, and counseling positions in universities, health care services, elementary and secondary schools, private industry, and government. Psychologists with a doctor of psychology (Psy.D.) degree have graduated from professional programs in psychology that emphasize coursework in abnormal psychology and diagnostic and treatment interventions; such practitioners are usually employed in clinical positions or in private practices, but they are becoming more numerous within university settings as well as in other areas of psychology.

A doctoral degree usually requires four to six years of graduate study. The Ph.D. degree culminates in a dissertation based on original research. Courses in quantitative research methods, which include the use of computer-based analysis, are an integral part of graduate study and are necessary to complete the dissertation. The Psy.D., however, may be based on practical work and examinations rather than a dissertation. In clinical or counseling psychology, the requirements for the doctoral degree usually include at least a one-year internship. Whichever degree you prefer to pursue, the challenging work toward the doctorate degree offers you the opportunity to integrate many high-level skills applicable to varied career opportunities and gives you the chance to be a leader within your setting.

TODAY'S MARKETPLACE

As implied throughout this chapter, the study of psychology offers broad training to fit varying interests and careers in today's ever-widening workplace. For instance, psychologists who focus on information technology integrate their expertise in human behavior to make sure that the next wave of computer technology is user-friendly or, for example, that pay-per-view technologies become simpler to use. Graduates from similar programs may focus their research skills in different directions, such as researching gang behavior or conducting marketing strategies. Acknowledging that flexibility is key to future careers, psychology programs are equipping students for a variety of careers, from academe to business and government.

Today's psychology programs promote thinking and training that gear students to discover their own niches in the wide-ranging fields of interest and public need. Course tracks in cognitive psychology, industrial and organizational psychology, and human factors give students a solid foundation in research methodology and psychology, so they can pursue either academic or applied work. Student graduates populate medical schools as well as university psychology departments. They are working for the National Aeronautics and Space Administration (NASA) or in the oil sector to telephone companies. And of course, the computer industry is scrambling for well-trained psychologists to promote applied uses of programs or to study computer design to promote ergonomic benefits.

The need for training that fits psychologists' diversifying careers has sparked several APA initiatives, including the Task Force for Non-Academic Employment of Scientific Psychologists, which examines growing careers in applied research. "The field of psychology is evolving from a mental health profession into a broader health, leadership and organizational profession," says Lee Hersch, Ph.D., the task force's chair. "Psychology's stakeholders—students, faculty and practitioners—need to gear themselves for the shift" (cited in Murray, 1998). The new marketplace calls for entrepreneurial students, updated training programs, and a field that touts its unique contributions in emerging arenas.

Psychologists with clinical training still have a strong foothold in mental health care practice, and those with research training can still find jobs in academe, but not as easily as they once could. Managed care, less government funding of psychologists' research, diminishing tenured professorships, and other marketplace changes are prompting many aspiring psychologists to seek training that prepares them for applied niches. Twenty years ago the largest single proportion of psychologists worked in academe, according to data from the National Science Foundation (NSF). Today the largest single proportion work for business and industry, and that includes incorporated private practice.

Findings do show, however, that the marketplace has been friendly to psychologists. Psychologists land jobs at higher rates than physicists, chemists, and other scientists, according to NSF surveys: With fewer jobs in academe, psychologists often find work elsewhere because their training prepares them to work with people in a variety of ways, not just with test tubes, says Barbara Gutek, Ph.D., a task force member and University of Arizona professor.

MARKETING YOUR SKILLS

Psychologists will increasingly find work in technology, forensics, criminal justice, business development, public policy, and neuroscience. Doctoral graduates are entering a world where the career professor or independent practitioner is less and less the norm. Psychologists today often juggle several part-time jobs and roles. They consult, run workshops, and launch their own businesses—nearly 20 percent of them are self-employed.

The best way to prove one's job worthiness is through practica and internships, says Marita Franzke, Ph.D. When she was halfway through her doctorate, she interned with U.S. West, the telecommunications company she now works for in Boulder, Colorado. To get the most out of the experience, she took a one-year leave of absence from her training program—enough time to make a strong impression on the company.

After she completed her dissertation on human-computer interaction, the company immediately snapped her up. Now Franzke works on making a host of technologies user-friendly—from voice mail, to Yellow Pages directories on the internet, to pay-per-view. "Stepping into a new project, quickly understanding where you can have the greatest impact, and then working with a team to achieve those goals makes the job fun and challenging," says Franzke (cited in Murray, 1998).

PROGRESSIVE TRAINING

Supportive training programs that emphasize internships and applied research are also key to finding less traditional jobs. Faculty that value and promote applied careers as much as preparation for more traditional academic careers are important in assisting students to fit the ever-changing needs of today's work environment. Programs that foster relationships with industry and brief their students on marketplace trends are at the forefront in assisting students in a competitive marketplace.

Departments of psychology that encourage students to take electives in such areas as management, education, and public policy and require students to gather portfolios that record their activities—internships, practica, program evaluations, or literature reviews—in a specialty area such as health or forensic psychology make the journey toward knowledge both challenging and practical. Such programs also promote students' presentation and teamwork skills to help them in the workplace. This approach helps today's students be proactive about recognizing marketplace forces and understand what makes them valuable to various organizations and to their communities at large. The next story describes how certain programs are combining dual interests that can lead students toward interesting career directions.

Brian H. Bornstein, Ph.D., who is professor of law psychology and cognitive programs at the University of Nebraska, characterizes many aspects in his decision to become a psychologist and describes the satisfaction he derives from working on a college campus. Also, in his career he has had the opportunity of combining two interests, psychology and law. Programs that provide an interaction of careers are at the forefront of psychological training for the twenty-first century.

∽ ——————————————————————————————————————

Combining Law and Psychology
Brian H. Bornstein

I never planned to be a psychologist, nor a university professor, until I became one. For starters, I didn't plan to major in psychology as an undergraduate. After going through several majors (some declared, some not), I wound up in psychology because I found the material inherently interesting, I had a couple of very stimulating professors who got me involved in their research, and the relatively undemanding requirements of the major gave me time to pursue other academic interests as well. My undergraduate honors research was even a study of feeding behavior in rats.

I went to graduate school because I liked research and wanted to keep doing it; but between college and grad school, I decided to switch from rats to humans because the research questions seemed more directly applicable to everyday life (this is not at all to suggest that the results of animal studies are not applicable, they're just usually more removed, and I guess I needed more immediate gratification of my empirical desires). So I started studying decision making, and stumbled into jury decision-making as a topic of study, partly to satisfy the frustrated law school aspirations I had had at one point in college, but mostly because it afforded a decision-making context with relatively well defined parameters and significant consequences for both the parties themselves and public policy.

In graduate school I didn't think much about jobs (and the faculty unfortunately didn't do much to counsel us on possible careers), but I gravitated toward academic positions as the easiest way for me to continue doing what I was doing and get paid for it. Coming out of a small experimental program, and studying decision making, I was stumped initially when all the job ads said they were looking for a (cognitive, social, developmental, etc.) psychologist; none said they wanted someone who studied decision making. So I applied for jobs in both cognitive and social psychology, and after two jobs as a cognitive psychologist (at Bucknell and Louisiana State Universities) I came to think of myself as one.

Part of being a cognitive psychologist meant teaching a course on memory, which led me to start conducting research on memory, which led me back to the law, this time in the context of research on eyewitness testimony. And now at midcareer I find myself well entrenched in the field of psychology and law, in one of the few programs devoted to that area, at the University of Nebraska.

There are two things that I find most satisfying about my job. First is the nearly total freedom to study and think about whatever I feel like, and to arrange my schedule as I see fit. I choose what to teach and when to teach it (within some departmental constraints). I choose what to research and how to investigate it. I don't have a boss in the traditional sense, and I can easily schedule work appointments around family responsibilities (or an occasional round of golf) if necessary.

Second are the students and, more broadly, living and working in a university setting. My daily interactions are nearly all with people (faculty, students, and administrators) who share many of my professional and personal interests. I am surrounded by a diverse group of fellow knowledge-seekers, who love to learn new stuff as much as I love to learn and share it. Students attend university, and faculty work at one, for a variety of reasons, but one major reason is to learn—through taking courses, teaching courses, and engaging in scholarship. I get a charge out of learning and helping others learn, and I can't imagine a better environment for doing that.

FOCUS ON CAREER QUESTIONS

Take time now to pause and ask the following questions: What do I want from my college experience? What do I want from my major? What do I want from my career? These are all complex questions, so don't feel discouraged if you can't come up with immediate answers. Just put the questions on the "back burner" as you review this book. What you learn here may guide you to the answers you seek.

If you've seriously reflected on your educational and career goals but remain unsure, make an appointment for career counseling at the Career Services Office on your campus. Also consider making an appointment at the Counseling Center to take occupational interest tests. Another option is to take time off from school to gain job experience. Then, once you know why you want to go to college, you should be much more interested in your classes and motivated to do well.

A final story by Frank Rath Jr., Ph.D., now a semi-retired military psychologist, shares many of this chapter's themes of circuitous routes to career decision making. Sometimes choices are made after discovering that you are not that interested in traditional school programs. Physical challenges are equally important, as well as invigorating, during your early career. Also, careers in the military, especially for those with backgrounds in psychology, offer a myriad of challenges not usually found in academic or clinical settings. Even within a military framework, finding the right niche for yourself comes through feedback from a variety of teachers and mentors who encourage your interests. Although practical concerns are important in a balanced lifestyle, the passion and excitement of learning about yourself and about how the world around you works is what really makes the study of psychology a key source of nourishment in final career plans.

ᗡ ───

Life as a Military Psychologist
Frank H. Rath Jr.

Even though I was fortunate to go through an excellent public school system in Garden City, Long Island, New York, I don't recall any offering of psychology courses. And I probably wouldn't have been attracted to them if they had been offered. My exposure to learning about people and behavior was largely through discussions in English literature courses and participation in the Lutheran Church.

When I matriculated at Dartmouth College in September 1960, my declared major was chemistry, a default choice as the more philosophical ambling that was to occur on campuses later was not tolerated. My freshman year included an introductory chemistry course that I didn't enjoy nor do well in (C+). I didn't take a psychology course until my sophomore year, when I took Introductory Psychology with several hundred other students, one of a handful of courses with a student enrollment of over twenty.

I had done well with my freshman grades and was then an honor's student and was assigned to a professor for individual readings, rather than a discussion group or lab, and that was a breakthrough experience. I recall reading one of Alfred Korzybski's works on structural differential and linguistic relativism and being fascinated by his thoughts. I was launched to an understanding of how our varied cultures influenced how we viewed, and interacted with, our world; a precursor to my later use of the Rorschach to understand individuals' perceptions of their world (Dr. Rath has taught Rorschach interpretation for many years to medical residents and psychology interns). For example, on Long Island we had snow, one kind only; the Eskimos had at least five different terms for different snows.

Although I didn't realize it at the time, I was to establish my two career identities at Dartmouth: U.S. Army officer and psychologist. I had enrolled in the Army's Reserve Officer Training Corps at the encouragement of my brother-in-law, then a newly commissioned 2nd Lieutenant who was familiar with Dartmouth's unique Mountain and Winter Warfare Program. In this program I was trained in downhill and cross-country skiing, as well as cliff climbing, repelling, and building rope bridges. At the same time I chose to major in psychology and most enjoyed the only two clinical courses offered and social psychology.

I can recall several key learning experiences at Dartmouth. One was in a social psychology lab in my junior or senior year. When I showed up first, the professor pulled me aside and asked me to be his stooge. Half the class would be debating the pros and cons of a long-since forgotten topic, and the other half would be observing and making notes behind one-way mirrors. I was to initially go with one side and gradually shift my opinion, seeing if the others would come along with me, which they did. When the professor and observers shared their observations with the assembled class, my former colleagues in agreement were not happy with me, feeling duped. I took home a powerful lesson about the indirect approach of joining with someone before trying to effect change, called as I later learned, "the therapeutic alliance."

Another key learning experience was working as the assistant to Professor Joseph de Rivera in a study regarding the recognition of facial expressions of certain emotions and relationships between the attitudes of parents and their teenage children about selected behaviors. I can remember the open discussions with Dr. de Rivera and a pleasant Sunday evening dinner at his home with his wife and two young children. I can also clearly remember having to show him the stains I had made by a liquid spill on the outer portions of several of the facial sketches; this was before the availability of photocopies, and I have subsequently been quite careful with my materials.

I was also influenced by the Army Reserved Officer Training Corps faculty. These included Master Sergeant William Brown, a veteran of the 10th Mountain Division in World War II, Majors Elmer Hassett and Francis Gross, both Korean War veterans, and Colonel Joseph Whitehorne, veteran of World War II and Korea.

Upon graduating from Dartmouth College in June 1964 and being commissioned as 2nd Lieutenant, Field Artillery, United States Army, I departed for Fort Sill, Oklahoma, and twelve weeks of Field Artillery Basic Officer's course. This was followed by Airborne training at Fort Benning, Georgia, where I managed to successfully complete the three-week course in spite of my aversion to heights. I was pleased to get through the multiple jumps out of the 34-foot towers, the one drop off the 250-foot tower, and the five jumps out of aircraft. I never jumped again.

In November 1965, while at Target Acquisition Officer's course (radar, sonar, etc.) at Fort Sill, I received orders for Vietnam. I first went to Fort Bragg, North Carolina, for five weeks of Military Assistance Training Advisor's training, taught mainly by Special Force's sergeants, and twelve weeks of Vietnamese-language instruction at the Defense Language Institute at the Presidio of Monterey, California.

In Vietnam I served on a district advisory team in the Mekong Delta of South Vietnam for twelve months. No electricity, no indoor plumbing, chickens and pigs roaming at will. We had three to five U.S. Army advisors embedded with the Vietnamese military and civilians. It was a profoundly interesting and informative experience. I got to know my American comrades and Vietnamese counterparts very well; there were no distractions but the war. I learned much about leadership and training from my boss, who went on to retire as a highly regarded major general. I also learned a lot from my counterpart, a Vietnamese 1st Lieutenant who was medically retired several years later from head wounds and in 1975 was put in a concentration camp for two and one-half years. He was a model of patience and dedication without one ounce of corruption. I was fortunate to have a reunion with him in March 2002 in Vietnam when I returned to look for him and other colleagues.

I was extended beyond my active duty obligation of three years because of the war and had to reapply to Syracuse University and the University of North Carolina at Chapel Hill a second time for the fall 1968 class after being accepted by both for the 1967 fall semester. I was interested in people and how they functioned. But I was not sure if clinical psychology was for me, and thus I chose not to remain on active duty and take advantage of the army's generous Graduate Student Program. A much-admired cousin had earned an MBA at Harvard School of Business and my backup plan was to go for an MBA if I didn't like clinical psychology.

My wife and I elected to go to UNC–Chapel Hill, based on its being a four-year versus a five-year program and that it was farther from our parents' homes in New Hampshire and Pennsylvania. We had a good relationship with our families but felt distance would not hurt our new marriage.

Starting graduate school in September 1968 was an anxiety-provoking experience. I had been away from academia for four years, and there was a palpably hostile climate toward military veterans. I soon got back in the groove of writing coherent papers and mastering material for exams. We were fortunate to have a faculty that had a real interest in teaching and development of our clinical and academic skills. I became hooked on clinical psychology because of the role models and early, extensive practicum experiences. I worked closely with the late Bill Eichmann, my dissertation chair and a World War II veteran whom I regret not talking with more about his wartime experiences, the late George Welsh, W. Grant Dahlstrom, M. David Galinsky, Nancy Robinson, and others.

So, I overcame the academic anxiety. The bias against veterans is another story. One of the first things I read in the department was an open letter signed by many (almost all?) of the clinical faculty opposing the Vietnam War. Over time it was clear that they did not personalize it to me, and I enjoyed warm relationships with all faculty. I was even selected for an award as the outstanding clinical graduate in 1972.

The student body was a different story. The draft was still in effect, and there were many men in the graduate school who had not fulfilled their military commitment, ranging from neighbors in student housing to classmates. I recall several things keenly.

First, we had a "T-group" (unstructured training group) facilitated by two psychologists not on the faculty in late September, early October of the first year. Participation was "voluntary" and we all volunteered. I think it was late on the first day when two of my thirteen classmates demanded to know what I had done in Vietnam (I had kept my Vietnam experiences to myself while my wife and I followed the war news with keen interest, having many American and Vietnamese friends still involved). I recall explaining the advisory role as being much like that of a psychology consultant (which it was), and as similar to the Peace Corps except in a war zone.

During the first year of graduate school I found that I missed the camaraderie of the army, and my wife Pat, a former army nurse, didn't object when I applied for and was accepted into the army's then Graduate Student Program. The program would pay my salary and allowances as a captain in exchange for four years of service after internship. While on active duty I did typical clinical activities; that is, assessment; individual, group, and marital and family therapy; consultation to health care professionals and military commanders; and responsibility for running three different psychology services and internship programs. I have many positive memories of helpful clinical interventions that I initiated and having the opportunity to train a large number of talented psychologists.

I was fortunate to have two fine mentors during that time, Colonels Chuck Thomas, Ph.D., and Bob Nichols, Ph.D. Colonel Thomas was shot down over France in World War II (he volunteered early and was trained as a pilot) and after completing his training in psychology served at several army posts before becoming the full-time psychology consultant to the army surgeon general. In the latter post he shaped the training and assignments of clinical psychologist to become more directly relevant to the training and operational needs of the military, rather than simply office practice. Bob Nichols was my internship chief of service and a public health–educated psychologist who nurtured a broader role for clinical psychology within the military.

The army offered some opportunities not typical of regular clinical office practice and I present two such examples. While I was chief of Psychology Services at William Beaumont Army Medical Center, El Paso, Texas, during the years 1974–1978, we occasionally worked with Vietnam veterans experiencing difficulties related to their wartime experiences. The relevant literature was scant at that time and often consisted of thinly veiled attacks against the Vietnam War and U.S. government. I did literature searches back to World War II and accumulated a fairly comprehensive set of articles and chapters. The Veterans Administration had not yet begun to offer outreach services to Vietnam veterans who had left active duty and been essentially rejected by their communities, that is, given no recognition for their sacrifices and no employment.

I was struck by the failure of the institution of the army to retain lessons learned from one conflict to another. By the time I was assigned to the 7th Medical Command, Heidelberg, Germany, in 1978 I was determined to do something to improve the army's readiness to effectively manage combat stress reactions in future conflicts, to both enhance combat strength and reduce risk for post-traumatic stress disorder.

I developed projections of the number of combat stress reaction soldiers who could be returned to duty if we were ready to execute the well-established principles of proximity, immediacy, and expectancy. I developed the concept of the combat effectiveness continuum that depathologized temporary ineffectiveness. With the late Larry Ingraham, an active duty social psychologist, I co-hosted a small two-day meeting that included a combat experienced officer, an organizational effectiveness officer, and a psychiatrist. After the meeting I wrote a sixteen-page, single-spaced summary that was forwarded by Major General Spencer Reid, Commander of 7th Medical Command, to Lieutenant General Charles Pixley, then army surgeon general. General Pixley responded, "Your report . . . has generated a great deal of interest throughout the AMEDD community. The Academy of Health Sciences in conjunction with the Health Sciences Command and the Walter Reed Army Institute of Research, is using this report to develop doctrine for a separate system to manage psychiatric casualties."

This action initiated the planning and support for the current U.S. Army combat stress control doctrine and resources that have been highly effective in retaining soldiers on duty who have experienced transient stress-related ineffectiveness while medically evacuating only those with likely psychiatric disorders. I am pleased that I was able to get the ball rolling!

I was to continue on active duty as an officer and psychologist until retiring as a lieutenant colonel in June 1989. Since that time, I have continued as a consultant at Walter Reed Army Medical Center, teaching the Rorschach and other personality instruments to new psychology interns, and enjoying the continual contact with staff and each year's medical resident class. I have also found time to work at the University of Maryland Medical School as a clinical associate professor of psychiatry, providing therapeutic services to an inner-city mental health clinic and offering supervision to interns and residents. Through these "retirement" years, I have also been offered contractual work at one of the national intelligence agencies and have worked part-time as a contract psychologist at the Office of Medical Services within the U.S. State Department performing assessments and offering recommendations on individuals ranging from those evacuated to the United States from overseas postings for psychiatric reasons to those whom Diplomatic Security identified as possible security risks.

A final role has been teaching at Walter Reed Army Medical Center for the past fifteen years. It has been a pleasure to teach and consult with the psychology residents, men and women who have gone on to serve in Korea, Afghanistan, Iraq, the Balkans, Germany, Italy, and throughout the United States. And it has been one super career as a psychologist in the military!

CHAPTER 3

Current Issues in Psychology

A DISCIPLINE WITH FAR-RANGING EFFECTS

Topics in psychology are ever widening in their quest to be relevant to today's students and to the world at large. As in any behavioral science, the number and variety of current and newer issues is infinite. As controversies are resolved satisfactorily, newer ones appear for discussion and examination. The merits of short-term versus long-term therapy, the benefits of research-based clinical applications to treatment of mood disorders, disparate views on psychologists prescribing medications, the continuing intrusion of politics into the health care system, how third-party insurance payments control the types of treatment prescribed and who will perform such procedures, and the mainstreaming of the mentally ill into communities, neighborhoods, and workplaces are just a few of today's hot topics. The psychological community grapples with these issues in the classroom as well as in the media, and further in their professional organizations and at scholarly and scientific meetings.

Dr. Pat DeLeon addresses these topics in the following paragraphs espousing the importance for psychologists to commit their time and expertise to influence public policy. He was a key advisor to Hawaii senator Daniel Inouye beginning in 1974. Besides his position as staffer on Capitol Hill, he has been instrumental in formulating policy for APA and served a term as its president.

Involvement in Shaping Public Policy
Pat DeLeon

Having been involved on a day-to-day basis in the public policy (i.e., political) process at the national level for slightly more than three decades, I believe without question that it is personally satisfying and professionally rewarding. I grew up in a family in which both parents were lawyers (my mother being the second female attorney in the history of the state of Connecticut) and active members of our local Democratic party. Had I first gone to law school (as my father wished), I would undoubtedly have become an elected official.

Although the majority of elected officials have a background in law (for example, 59 percent of the U.S. Senate), I have found over the years that my training in psychology has provided me with a very useful and often unique perspective. In so many ways, the behavioral sciences are the key to effectively addressing a wide range of society's pressing priorities—in the health, education, employment, and numerous other arenas. What are teenage violence and school dropouts, if not behavioral issues? Study after study has stressed the all important psychosocial-cultural-economic gradient of quality health care that, I would suggest, is the purview of the behavioral sciences. Similarly, prevention is, without question, the key to addressing individual and societal health disparities.

Psychology is a steadily maturing profession, in both numbers and scope of influence. Psychologist John Gardner served as secretary of the then Department of Health, Education, and Welfare (HEW) under President Lyndon Johnson. Colleen Hacker was the mental skills coach for the extraordinarily successful Women's Olympic Soccer Team. Former APA president Phil Zimbardo conducted the historic Stanford prisoner studies.

The policy discussions now occurring within professional psychology are qualitatively different than they were a decade ago. We are developing innovative postdoctoral programs in psychopharmacology, geropsychology, and health psychology—all targeted toward society's newest priorities. Collectively, we are actively involved in developing cost-effective, behavioral-based telehealth initiatives. And highly constructive efforts are underway at our highest association governance level to ensure that the composition of psychology will reflect the demographic and cultural-ethnic changes evolving within society as a whole. Our graduate student organization (APAGS) currently has over 59,000 members. Having been personally involved in the governance of the APA for approximately a quarter of a century, and ultimately having the opportunity in 2000 to serve as APA president, it has been exciting to help shape these changes.

One of the most critical nuances of thinking like a psychologist—one's first professional discipline truly does shape how one views the world—is a deep appreciation for individual differences and the need for experimentally testing out "what we surely know." And that one individual can make a real difference. Children, for example, are considerably more than "little adults," notwithstanding how they might be treated by health care administrators and clinicians.

Accordingly, it is very satisfying that efforts made more than two decades ago have resulted in the establishment of a special Pediatric Emergency Medical Service demonstration program; that psychology's forensic expertise has been provided the same recognition as that of medicine throughout our federal courts, thus fundamentally changing an individual's right to a fair trial; that girls and women can excel in science, not withstanding society's bias; and that a new generation of American Indian and Native Hawaiian psychologists are steadily seeking to improve the quality of life of their people. Systematically bringing psychological expertise to the public policy process does make a real difference in the lives of our nation's citizens. And it can be fun.

One professor who believes in this need to generalize the skills of a psychologist for the betterment of society is William Crain, Ph.D., from the City College of New York, who has viewed the changing environment within the public school system as a detriment to his children as well as to other students facing a culture of assessment over education. He was able to channel his frustrations through running for elected office at his local school board. His story emphasizes the call for psychologists to begin making an impact on the relevant issues of society. His views and description of his concerns are related in the following story.

Challenging the School System
William Crain

Our children began attending public elementary schools in Teaneck, New Jersey—a large suburb of New York City—in the mid-1970s. The school system had an excellent reputation, but our children didn't like school very much. When I talked to other children and adults, I found that a dislike of school was commonplace—both within our community and outside it. Many parents told me that their children had begun life curious and eager to learn, but after a few years of school, their enthusiasm had faded.

Soon the standards and testing movement got underway, and I saw children becoming unhappier yet. Schools throughout the nation began introducing formal academic instruction in the very early grades—even in kindergarten—leaving the young children confused and distraught. Moreover, children of all ages were spending more and more time preparing for standardized tests, and they found this instruction very tedious. They also dreaded the tests themselves.

In 1987, I decided to run for election to the Teaneck school board to try to address the problem at the local level. During the campaign, I talked to many parents and educators about making learning a more rewarding experience. But I consistently ran into a stern objection. Joyful learning might be nice, people said, but the main goal of education is to prepare children for a competitive future. Children must master the skills they need to get into the best colleges and compete in the adult world. Mastering these skills might not be much fun, but it's necessary for future success.

That election campaign forced me to think hard about the goals of education and my own perspective as a developmental psychologist. I reflected on developmental scholars who had most impressed me—writers such as Rousseau, Piaget, Montessori, and Elkind—and tried to articulate my position as clearly as I could. Basically, my message was this.

We, as adults, do need to pay some attention to what children need for the future. But when we focus too exclusively on the future, we overlook the way children naturally grow and learn. Children are inwardly motivated to develop different capacities at different times, and they need activities that enable them to develop their naturally emerging capacities at their present phase. When they find such activities, they work on them with great enthusiasm and concentration. And when they are finished, they are often happy and at peace, for they have had a chance to develop something vital within themselves. If we want children to develop fully, then, we cannot just give them the tasks we consider important for their future, but tasks they find most meaningful in their present lives.

A particular issue during that campaign was the proposal to shift from a half day to a full day kindergarten. I argued that we should not make the change in order to introduce more academic instruction. Five-year-olds are generally at a phase when they naturally develop through play, artistic activities, and the exploration of nature—not formal academic lessons. Although it is tempting to start them on the academic skills they will need in the years ahead, it is more important to give them the opportunities to develop their natural potentials at their own phase of development.

I found it particularly helpful to emphasize children's emotions and attitudes toward learning. When we give children tasks that meet our own goals and concerns about the future, the children often find the tasks dull and tedious. They don't approach the tasks with energy or think deeply about them. When, in contrast, we give children tasks they find meaningful in their present lives, they think fully and imaginatively, and their minds expand. And they look forward to further learning. Ultimately, this enthusiasm for learning often leads to the greatest academic achievement.

When the votes were tallied, I lost my bid for election. But I received a respectable number of votes, and the next year I won a seat on the school board. I served on the board for nine years. During that time, I took up many causes, and I had a few successes. I was able to help fend off some excessive pressures on children. I also helped protect some of my region's natural settings, which children need to learn and grow.

But as a voting board member, I lost more often than not. And the standards and testing movement continued to grow—both in my community and nationwide. Still, when I left the board, I felt I had made a difference. Beyond the particular school board decisions, I contributed a developmental perspective to the ongoing educational dialogue. My school board experiences also deepened my understanding of educational issues and informed my later writing. I look back on the 1987 election campaign, my initial venture into school politics, with satisfaction.

Psychology's relevance is seen through the changing landscape on college campuses. More freedom of expression, more comfort within a diverse population, and more research areas are explored than ever before. Psychology is truly a dynamic discipline that is in touch with changing needs of a changing society. The next story by Professor Esther Rothblum of San Diego State University explores the issues of gender identity and how she was able to incorporate her skills and interests to expand psychology's exploration and acceptance of individual differences.

Gay and Lesbian Issues
Esther D. Rothblum

Carol Gilligan has described the marked changes in girls' development as they become interested in boys and lose their sense of self (Gilligan, 1993). That certainly does not describe the experience of lesbian girls. I couldn't be part of the popular clique in high school as I had no interest in dating boys, so instead I focused on academics. When it was time for college, my father consulted his best friend, a college professor, for some reputable "girls' schools" and that's how I ended up at Smith College.

It was wonderful to see college women rather than men in all the leadership positions, and I thrived on the presence of this women's community. In contrast, my graduate school had mostly male faculty, who tended to select male graduate students for funded research placements. There were three female graduate students in my class, and no one seemed to be able to tell us apart even though our names and appearances were quite different. But my Smith College experience gave me the resilience to make it through, and I feel strongly that all women should have the luxury of a female-only education at some point in their lives.

I was doing my research on depression, focusing on ways to improve assessment and diagnosis before the third edition of the *Diagnostic and Statistical Manual of Mental Disorders* came out and standardized these issues. One day at a social event at my clinical internship in 1979, a woman in my class stated that she was studying agoraphobia, and had noticed that most of her clients and research participants were women. Another woman remarked that, interestingly, she too had noticed that the majority of her participants in her eating disorder research were female. That is when it first occurred to me that most of my own depressed clients and research participants were women. These students and I presented a panel about mental health disorders in which women predominate, and then I co-edited a book on this topic. One of our male faculty members remarked, "Don't study women; it's too narrow a subject." This was a recurrent theme, with well-meaning mentors trying to talk me out of such a radical career goal. "You'll never find a job," was their standard advice when they heard I was co-editing a book about women as a graduate student about to enter the academic marketplace.

I did a postdoctoral fellowship at Yale University; my mentor, a depression researcher, was the only woman who was tenured at the Yale Medical School at that time. She was quite concerned about my feminism, probably fearing (with good reason) that her laboratory would get a negative reputation among her peers.

Interestingly, when I was offered a tenure-track job at the University of Vermont, it was based on the fact that the clinical program was placed on probation by the APA for having no female faculty members. As soon as I arrived in Vermont, the male faculty members were eager for me to do something, anything, on women, just so they could get the program off probation. So I had carte blanche to do research on women's mental health, teach a course on the psychology of women, and mentor our mostly female students about women's issues. I became editor of the journal *Women & Therapy*. In the early 1980s there was little information about gender; it was even hard to publish research in the available academic journals. Being a journal editor meant I could invite feminist academics, theorists, and practitioners to write about many topics never before covered in the psychological literature.

A senior member of my department was on an APA board that appointed psychologists to various committees. He suggested my name for the Committee on Lesbian, Gay, and Bisexual Concerns. At that time I had done no research or writing on lesbian issues, so I felt like an imposter serving on this committee. To compensate, I plunged into research about lesbians, focusing mostly on methodological challenges when dealing with a hidden and marginalized population.

Interestingly, doing research about lesbians in the late 1980s never had the negative stigma that doing research about women had just a decade earlier. Even today, I continue to study lesbian issues. My current research focuses on using heterosexual siblings as a demographic comparison group for lesbians, gay men, and bisexuals. When Vermont was the first state to legalize same-sex relationships, I compared same-sex couples who had these civil unions during the first year of the new legislation with same-sex couples in their friendship circle who had not had civil unions, and with heterosexual married siblings and spouses. I also edit the *Journal of Lesbian Studies* that is interdisciplinary, so I keep informed about lesbian issues in the humanities, fine arts, and sciences as well as the social sciences.

In sum, I would urge students to follow their heart when choosing a career path and not the advice of family members or academic mentors. Now that I have observed career paths of our own graduate students for over two decades, I notice that the ones who work with well-known faculty and continue in the research paths of these individuals are not always the most successful academics. Some of our most oppositional students, who never seemed to fit in well with graduate school, go on to develop cutting-edge theories and research programs. I personally feel that when something begins to look good on my academic resume, it is time to move on to other things!

RESPONDING TO SOCIETY'S NEEDS

In today's world, health practitioners are continually expanding their focus and knowledge on mental health issues. They have finally acknowledged that mental health concerns are truly "real" and that disorders of the mind interfere with daily health and happiness (Oster & Montgomery, 1994). Finally, physicians and other allied health professionals have discovered that emotionally and neurologically based disorders, including depression, eating disorders, bipolar illness, anxiety, attention deficit disorder, and Alzheimer's diseases, have all been shown to be as significant as cancer and heart disease in terms of premature death and lost productivity. The discipline of psychology has been at the forefront in disseminating information to overcome the barriers to accessing help. Through the research and clinical efforts of many psychologists and their ability to communicate these findings to the general public, society is quickly becoming a sophisticated consumer of mental health interventions.

Psychology's understanding of society's health and mental health needs is also becoming increasingly more sophisticated, and with that knowledge there exist increased opportunities for treatment providers and other skilled professions related to the discipline of psychology. For example, it seems that every day there is news about varying childhood disorders. From sleep problems to tantrums to obsessive-compulsive disorder to attention-deficit/ hyperactivity disorder, psychological programs promote the theoretical, research-based, and clinical intervention skills that improve the outcome for children and their families. One such practitioner, Mack Stephenson, Ph.D., who is a licensed psychologist with a specialization in assessing and treating behavioral and developmental disorders in children, has worked extensively in the neuropsychology and autistic spectrum diagnostic clinics at Harvard Medical School/Children's Hospital. He also ran the federal Early Intervention Program and spent three years overseeing all psychology services in Japan for active U.S. Navy personnel. Certainly, the field of psychology is expanding and psychology graduates fit into many niches.

Another interesting story demonstrating how a career in psychology can be satisfying on many levels is written by a professor from a Psy.D. program (that is, a professional psychology practitioner school that culminates in providing doctorate in psychology degrees). These programs emphasize applied work for graduate students as opposed to focusing on research skills. Students from these programs gain early supervised experiences to deal effectively with a variety of everyday mental health problems seen in hospitals and clinics. They also learn up-to-date psychological theories to understand these disorders and gain the necessary clinical skills to counteract the symptoms presented to them.

Michelle Nealon-Woods, Psy.D., received her degree from the Chicago School of Professional Psychology in 2001. In spring 2002 she returned to the Chicago School to teach as adjunct faculty and in fall 2003 began as an assistant professor. She specializes in the treatment of children, adolescents, and their families. Her scholarly interests include the development and improvement of treatment interventions for children and adolescents, particularly focused on improving the application of clinical approaches with diverse populations.

Balancing Work and Family
Michelle Nealon-Woods

My career as a clinical psychologist began in Dublin, Ireland, where I completed my first master's degree at University College Dublin. From there, I was invited to study at the Queen's University of Belfast, Northern Ireland, where I had my first formal training as a practicing clinical psychologist.

I left the program at Queen's University of Belfast as I knew I was moving to the United States and little of my degree there would transfer to American psychology programs. While researching the different university-based and professional schools, I was sold on the Chicago School of Professional Psychology because of its emphasis on multicultural education and training and because of its very strong emphasis on training the practitioner. Since my enrolment in the Chicago School, I have remained completely committed to the professional school model of education and training.

The world of professional psychology has been where I found my career home. I graduated from the Chicago School in 2001, and while working on my postdoctoral residency I began teaching as an adjunct professor at the Chicago School, focusing initially on behavioral models and therapies. In 2003, I joined the Chicago School as program faculty for the Doctor of Psychology Program and have never once looked back! I now continue to teach intervention courses, such as Basic Intervention: Cognitive-Behavioral and Advanced Intervention: Cognitive. In addition, I teach professional development seminars and have been able to teach courses in life span development and a seminar in child and adolescent therapy.

Although I had identified teaching and mentoring students as primary career goals, I could never have estimated the extent to which I would enjoy these activities. What has been most rewarding about my teaching activities is the range of student contact I am afforded on a daily basis. In addition to in-classroom teaching, my responsibilities include student advising, student mentorship, curriculum development, committee membership, community work and consultation, interviewing applicants for the Doctor of Psychology Program, chairing dissertation work, giving conference presentations, supervising students on clinical practicum, and much more.

In addition to my work at the Chicago School, I work one day a week in private practice, mostly with children, adolescents, and their families. My clinical work reminds me daily of the reasons I aspired to be a clinical psychologist. The potential impact (through empirically based interventions) we have on clients never ceases to motivate me to become a better clinician. The complexities of human life and human experiences, and my ability to share these in the classroom, add a richness to teaching that students comment about on a regular basis.

Outside of my career, I am a mother. Being a working mother has its challenges, and maintaining a healthy sense of personal and professional balance has been one of my great life lessons. The combination of teaching and private practice has afforded me the flexibility I need to pursue both a career and a family. For those interested in pursuing clinical psychology as a profession, I would say to you that the art and science of psychology prepares us for more than just our careers. It is a life-long journey that evolves with the profession itself, and with those actively involved with the profession. These are lessons we learn as we take time to evolve into professional clinical psychologists, lessons I would encourage all never to rush but mindfully explore as you begin your graduate studies.

PSYCHOLOGY: A FUTURE OF CHANGE

Psychology is a science of great fertility, exploration, and dynamic change. Not only does psychology keep finding new areas of exploration, but new careers continue to appear as disciplines overlap and cross-disciplinary projects appear. Many psychologists work outside traditional psychology programs, such as in departments of neurology or special education. They find the skills they possess can be applied in many areas of applied research and clinical intervention. One such story is told by one of my former classmates from Middle Tennessee State University and Virginia Commonwealth University. Although our paths intertwined continuously throughout graduate school during our master's and doctoral programs, our separate skills, personal interests, and career directions separated us. Here Thomas Prohaska, Ph.D., from the University of Illinois, Chicago shares an alternative direction for psychology majors. His ultimate career path found him working in a department of public health. This choice allowed him to go in a direction that was important for society (gerontology), as well as one that was just beginning when he left graduate school.

An Alternative Career in Psychology: Public Health
Thomas R. Prohaska

Upon completing my postdoctoral training at the University of Wisconsin (after receiving my Ph.D. at Virginia Commonwealth University) that combined health psychology and gerontology, I had planned a traditional academic career in psychology. While I was going through the process of applying to psychology faculty positions, someone (I wish I could give credit to a specific person) suggested that I consider public health. I had no idea at the time what public health was or why they would be interested in psychologists who studied the aging process. I was fortunate enough to get into a field that was still in its very early development—gerontological public health.

Public health and psychology have a lot in common, especially the applied areas of behavior change. Behavioral scientists in public health often start out as psychologists or sociologists. They then combine their past training with that of other individuals in medically related disciplines such as health education, psychosocial epidemiology, and environmental health. However, by coming together as public health researchers and practitioners, they share important characteristics. These traits include a broad ecological approach to health problems in populations, an orientation to multidisciplinary population-based approaches to addressing the health in individuals, and instead of taking a one-on-one clinical approach, they focus on targeted populations for intervention. Another common characteristic to their work is that they strive to address a health issue prior to or early in its development through primary and secondary prevention rather than when a person's health is already compromised.

Psychologists in gerontological public health work in a very wide array of health issues, including promoting health behaviors known to be protective against chronic illnesses and disability, identifying behavioral risk factors for falls, and promoting favorable beliefs and attitudes toward health behaviors such as physical activity, smoking cessation, and appropriate diet. Many of the theoretical models used in this work have their basis in psychological theories, only applied to populations. Understanding the dynamics of doctor–older patient interactions leading to favorable health outcomes is based, in part, on principles from psychology including group interactions, learned helplessness, and attribution theory. Even the research methodology includes elements well known to research psychologists.

One of the most rewarding aspects of my work is that it can make a difference in the health and well-being of older adults, and sooner rather than later. While public health researchers publish in the same scientific journals as psychologists and other health professionals, such as *Health Psychology*, *Journal of Gerontology*, *American Journal of Public Health*, and the *Journal of the American Medical Association*, we also have a direct influence on the health of the public. Public health extends considerably farther than advancing the science—our real objective is to take the lessons learned from the science and make lasting positive changes in the health of the public as soon as possible. One of the most rewarding aspects of a career in public health for me is to see the research influence how we promote and protect the health of older adults and the effect of our work on health policy and community change.

ROLES OF PSYCHOLOGISTS

Because of the continually expanding incorporation of new ideas in psychology, trained psychologists now fill many roles in today's society. They are researchers, teachers, service providers (assessing needs, providing treatment), administrators (hospitals, government agencies, schools), and consultants (advising on problems in organizations, designing survey, and organizing new patient systems). They vary in their interests as well as their lifestyles.

RESEARCH

Some of the most important findings about human nature have come from the work of psychological researchers. Many psychological researchers are employed in university settings. In addition to engaging in research, many are also involved in teaching and mentoring the next generation of students. Psychologists research a huge number of topics ranging from anxiety and post-traumatic stress disorders in children to the best ways to increase attendance in an organization. They are passionate about their interests and conduct their research with equal zeal.

Psychologists also work as full-time researchers for organizations other than universities. These individuals are often employed by companies to study various research topics. The Army Research Institute (ARI), for example, frequently hires psychologists to investigate topics such as leadership performance and training evaluation. Other research psychologists might work for private companies who design experiments to test the effects of drugs on the behavior of patients or conduct survey research on topics of marketing preferences.

The following story describes one university professor's quest for understanding depression. Through his own applied work, as well as training with some of the most influential theorists, clinicians, and researchers in the field, Dr. Steven Hollon from Vanderbilt University has been able to produce a compilation of research issues that target one of the most common and most lethal of mental health disorders. By contributing to the scientific literature in conducting research and by disseminating this information to practitioners as well as students, he leaves a solid legacy and has gained much career satisfaction.

Depression Research
Steven D. Hollon

I have a long-standing interest in depression that has guided my work in teaching and research through the better part of my career. Before I ever got interested in psychology, I was interested in ethology and was intrigued that something like depression could be found so clearly in other species besides our own. I also was intrigued by the fact that some of the historical figures that I most admired, like Churchill and Lincoln, had personal histories of depression.

During my graduate training at Florida State University, I became interested in the work of Aaron Beck, M.D., on cognitive models of depression and Martin Seligman, Ph.D., on learned helplessness. I got in touch with both and was able to do my clinical internship year in Philadelphia. I worked primarily with Beck and his colleagues as they did their early work on cognitive therapy with depression and got a chance to sit in with Seligman and his research group as they did their attributional reformulation of the helplessness model.

These experiences were invaluable and set the stage for all work that I have done in the ensuing years—Beck for clinical innovation and the importance of exploring patient phenomenology and Seligman for experimental psychopathology. I also had the chance to meet and talk with Gerald Klerman, M.D. (now deceased, but then at Harvard), from whom I modeled the importance of clinical trials.

I have a strong interest in clinical issues, both the etiology of depression and its treatment. In my experience, the most efficacious clinicians I have known (like Beck) are those people who think the most powerfully theoretically about the phenomena they encounter clinically, and the most interesting research scientists (like Seligman) are those who study the mechanisms underlying issues of truly clinical import. I also came to believe (like Klerman) that anything that can be done clinically can and should be tested.

Throughout my career I have been interested in not only where depression comes from but what you have to do to treat it. My studies often have focused on comparisons between cognitive therapy and medications. Drugs represent the current standard of treatment; given my interest in a relatively novel approach like cognitive therapy, it made sense to compare it against the best the field had to offer. Moreover, as efficacious as the medications have typically been, there is no evidence that they do anything to reduce risk once their use is discontinued. That made them a perfect control for efforts to determine whether cognitive therapy truly had an enduring effect.

Studies by me and others suggest that cognitive therapy is at least as efficacious as medication treatment with all but the most severely depressed and psychotic patients. Moreover, these studies have consistently shown that cognitive therapy can reduce subsequent risk. That is, patients treated to remission with cognitive therapy are only about half as likely to relapse following treatment termination as patients treated to remission with medications alone.

It remains to be seen whether cognitive therapy will prevent the onset of wholly new episodes (recurrence), but indications from existing studies suggest that that might be the case. We have a study currently underway to look for just such an effect! Combined with indications that interventions based on cognitive therapy can be used to prevent initial onset in people at risk who have not yet been depressed, these studies suggest that people learn something in cognitive therapy that serves to offset factors that would otherwise put them at risk for depression. That should prove to be a major boon in a disorder that is highly recurrent.

My career has been an absolute delight. I have had the good fortune to work with some of the leading figures in the field and to work with students who have or will become the leaders of the future. I go to work each day with a real sense of enthusiasm and excitement; work has often been challenging, but it has always seemed important.

I have an intense dislike for depression and a great appreciation and affection for the people who tend to get depressed. I like to think that in some small way my efforts have contributed to our efforts to learn more about depression and how it can be treated and prevented. It has been a great and grand adventure and one that I hope to continue for as long as I may live.

TEACHING

College teaching is one of the most frequently chosen careers of psychologists. In fact, one survey found that close to one-third of all psychologists work at a college or university. A majority of college and university teachers have Ph.D. degrees. Psychologists with master's degrees are typically employed at two-year or community colleges.

Academia offers psychologists the opportunity to teach a host of different subjects to students. In the same way that many career paths exist for psychologists, so do the choices of subjects to teach. A curriculum of courses in psychology may include topics ranging from child therapy to experimental and cognitive psychology, forensic assessment, neuropsychology, animal learning, psychology of aging, and hypnotherapy. The following examples of career teaching demonstrate how much satisfaction may be gained in this career direction.

Studying Memory and Language
Lise Abrams

Although I have been a professor for only eight years at the University of Florida, I can already see how this path will become my life-long career. I am a cognitive psychologist studying the relationship between memory and language processes in young and older adults, with the broader goal of understanding why certain aspects of language and memory functioning are impaired in old age, whereas others remain intact. Both research and teaching have played an important role in my job satisfaction.

With respect to research, I have enjoyed watching my research program develop and feeling that my research can make a significant impact, not only in the academic community but also in people's lives. For example, I study tip-of-the-tongue (TOT) states, which are memory failures that occur when people are unable to recall a word that they are certain they know. TOT states increase as we get older, and older adults find these experiences to be particularly frustrating. By studying the causes of TOT states and the factors that can reduce them, I hope to improve older adults' conversational interactions, which can be disrupted by TOT states.

I also take great pride in mentoring students in research, which is a priority for me because of my own training. I became a cognitive psychologist because of my undergraduate and graduate mentors, who developed my enthusiasm in research and showed me the excitement of furthering science through my research. I have enjoyed disseminating those values to my own students.

I am also committed to serving as a role model for women students, to show them that an academic research career is an achievable goal for women. Although my research is a significant part of my career, I also love teaching, and I am proud of being a challenging teacher who develops students' capacities for abstract thinking and reasoning. I find gratification in seeing students learn, question, and discover the excitement of a field like cognitive psychology that is constantly changing and has ample room for exploration.

Creating Latino Mentoring Programs
Gustavo Carlo

Many of the relationships I have formed have been directly tied to my teaching at the University of Nebraska–Lincoln. Teaching is certainly one of the most visible and engaging activities. There is much to be said for the experiences in classrooms and in non-classrooms (e.g., research laboratories) that help foster reciprocal learning and positive long-term relationships. As a developmental psychologist, I find nothing more rewarding than to observe the positive transformation of undergraduate and graduate students. Graduation from college is but a rite of passage—growth and development continues and, for some of my students, my relationship with them continues to evolve. Although most people think of teaching when they think of a professor of psychology, teaching is only one venue that brings fulfillment and pride.

Other aspects of academia are less visible but equally satisfying. Oftentimes, you can provide unique resources (e.g., valuable information, expertise) to your community through research. In addition to enjoying university teaching experiences, I often speak at local community agencies, churches, schools, and other organizations. In addition, various community organizations ask me to consult on community program projects. My hope is that some of my research activities can lead to discoveries that may prove useful to researchers, practitioners, and policymakers.

One of my deepest convictions was to develop a research-based program that could help families directly. Recently, I had the opportunity to work with a group of scholars and community professionals to create a Latino youth–mentoring program (the Latino Achievement Mentoring Program; LAMP) in Lincoln, Nebraska. LAMP was developed to address the growing educational needs of Latino youth in our state. As co–program manager and one of the founders of LAMP, I work closely with our staff and the community to research new ways of improving the program. The personal rewards are numerous, but they stem directly from my interactions with the parents, children, school staffs, and colleagues. The program is a powerful example of the combined potential power of university and community collaboration to directly improve the quality of life for our community. Although I have observed or experienced some of the negativism in our society, most of the people I have met through my work experiences reinforce my belief that people have a strong, inner desire to better themselves and their world.

Variety and Flexibility as a Faculty Member
Steven Prentice-Dunn

As professor at the University of Alabama, I value two aspects of my job above all else: variety and flexibility. These qualities have allowed me to adjust my activities over time to reflect my changing interests and family commitments.

All faculty members are expected to teach, conduct research, and perform service. Although the balance of these tasks differs across campuses, faculty have the freedom to determine where to place the emphasis. For example, at the start of my career I was a dedicated researcher who was thrilled with designing and conducting studies for publication. I enjoyed producing the scientific results used by others. During those years I regarded teaching as a bit of a chore. I presented well-organized lectures but received little feedback from my classes.

One day I expressed my frustration to a friend who suggested that I try more active teaching methods such as discussions, demonstrations, and in-class writing assignments. From the first time I tried those techniques, a tremendous wave of energy was released in the class. I quickly realized that not only were students learning more but they were teaching me as well. Teaching quickly became a joy for me. Being a university professor has thus allowed me to explore ways to effectively teach while still conducting research and performing service at a reduced level. As my interests have changed, so too has my work.

In addition to providing variety, faculty jobs are flexible. Many Americans experience stress at trying to balance work and family. As a professor, I have not faced those challenges to the same degree. While some of my work must be done within the confines of typical business hours, much can be completed at my convenience. Such flexibility enabled me to actively participate in raising my two children. When sickness struck or when a school trip was planned, I was able to be there. When my kids expressed interest in seeing other areas of the country, our family was able to take long camping trips to explore those places.

Although my career has been fulfilling, some experiences stand out. As a beginning researcher, I studied the thoughts and emotions of people in groups. Much of that was conducted in a laboratory setting where variables could be tightly controlled. Imagine my surprise when several studies were introduced in South African courts to explain the behavior of specific people in a political demonstration. That experience taught me vividly that laboratory findings can speak to what happens in our everyday lives.

In recent years I have created brief interventions to encourage people to protect their health. Through lectures, pamphlets, videos, and discussions, my colleagues and I have sought to convince participants to attend cancer screenings, reduce exposure to the sun, begin regular breast self-examinations, and so forth. I am especially gratified to hear from former participants whose health has been preserved by behaviors that we have recommended (such as having suspicious skin spots checked by a dermatologist).

Memorable experiences are not limited to research. As a teacher, I have been moved by a nod of recognition as I spoke on some topic or a look of excitement upon someone seeing for the first time the link between two seemingly different concepts. I treasure the occasional e-mails from former students who tell me of situations where they applied lessons learned in my course.

Now that my children have begun college and no longer live at home, I again have adjustments to make at home and at work. I am fortunate to work in a setting where individual choices are allowed, where a variety of tasks can be done daily, and where one is surrounded year after year by interesting people.

THE WORLD OF SOCIAL PSYCHOLOGY

As mentioned throughout this book, the discipline of psychology explores many areas of the personal and interpersonal world. Psychologists explore brain-behavior relationships, as well as learning styles within the classroom. Psychologists also create and advocate for the culturally responsive delivery of mental health services, in addition to promoting substance abuse education. There are symposia within psychology that examine psychological intervention tools for deploying and redeploying soldiers during conflicts and investigating the therapeutic factors in group counseling.

One such subdiscipline in psychology, social psychology, is popular among students because of its application to everyday, real-life concerns and explorations. Social psychologists examine people's interactions with others and with the social environment. People with backgrounds in social psychology often work in organizational consultation, marketing research, systems design, or other applied psychology fields. Prominent areas of study include group behavior, leadership, attitudes, and perception. The following professors of social psychology—Ellen Langer, Ph.D., and Donelson Forsyth, Ph.D.—share their interests in this field. Through their passions they entice the reader with what they believe is "the true nature of psychology." Dr. Langer, from Harvard, has authored the best-selling books *Mindfulness* and *The Power of Mindful Learning*, while Dr. Forsyth received many "outstanding teacher" awards at Virginia Commonwealth University before recently moving to the University of Richmond to focus on ethical leadership.

Training as a Social Psychologist
Ellen J. Langer

Training as a psychologist, especially a social psychologist, cannot help but have a powerful impact on our lives. The effect on my own life has been immeasurable. This is the case for at least three reasons.

First, social psychology, in its concern for the impact of the situation or context on behavior, tends to look for interactions. That is to say, rather than expect that any influence will affect us in only one way, we learn early on to see that the influence is unlikely to affect us the same way across situations. So, for example, we may learn information by memorizing it for an exam, and we may do well on the exam. If, on the other hand, the exam asked us to use that information in a novel way and we learned it by mindlessly memorizing it, we would be less likely to do well on the exam. The "golden rule" of the field is "it depends." Searching for how and on what "it depends" keeps me engaged, allows me to take advantage of opportunities that otherwise would not be noticed, and helps me avert the danger not yet arisen. That is, mindful learning promotes effectiveness and creativity in all facets of my life.

Second, with its emphasis on the experimental method, social psychological training makes us aware of alternative explanations for everyday events. In any experiment, the researcher's task is in part to consider multiple possible causes and uncover which are most likely to be true. After conducting numerous experimental investigations we can't help but think this way regarding our own lives. As a result, when we experience negative outcomes we can easily think of several reasons why they may have occurred. The end result is a buffer to self-esteem and a more flattering view of other people as well. Both enhance performance in virtually all situations. Indeed, recognizing the potential of multiple causes helps me stay mindful. My own research has shown that mindfulness is good for psychological and physical health.

Third, by focusing on people's behavior as a result of situational factors, I've come to be aware that much of what is taken to be absolute is in fact malleable. So, for example, when presented with "facts," I've come to see them as "situated truths." That is, I recognize that the world is largely, if not totally, a social construction. Even with respect to art, which is said to be subjective, people respond as if there are absolute evaluations that are inherently true. This realization has come to free me to begin to paint. With no training, I've found a new creative outlet that has allowed me to reinvent myself. It results from mindfulness and increases my mindfulness. And, perhaps not surprisingly, painting gives me new ideas about behavior and leads me back to research.

My training has led me to do research that has been concerned with people's well-being and health. Early work on the importance for adults and the elderly of feeling control over their personal and interpersonal worlds, ways of reducing stress, how mindfulness is available and important for every aspect of our lives, to how a new creative activity can set the stage for dramatically increasing more generally, our mindful creativity, has, without question, enriched my own life.

Exploring Group Behavior
Donelson R. Forsyth

When I worked for a construction company in the 1970s, I spent many a lunch hour talking with the veterans about their experiences working all kinds of jobs. They had clear opinions about which jobs to avoid and which ones to seek. Avoid, they recommended, road crewing during the summer months in Florida. Keep away from "call backs," where the boss sends you

out to correct problems caused by other employees. Seek, instead, jobs that
are done in the shop or ones that required the use of heavy equipment. Such
jobs were always described with the catch phrase "good work, if you can
get it."

When I migrated from the world of construction and took a position as a
college professor and social psychologist, I found myself on the right side of
the "good work if you can get it" divide. Granted, professoring is still work.
There are politics of the office, bosses who make demands, and duties that
must be fulfilled. Nor is it a glamorous occupation, as Hollywood's depic-
tions of Indiana Jones–like professorial types would suggest. But depending
on one's goals and perspectives, it is a personally fulfilling pursuit. It is an
elite profession that requires special training and skill, and for much of the
time it feels more like a "calling" than "work," for it involves (a) learning and
practicing the skills valued by the profession; (b) seeking immersion in a
community whose members are similarly dedicated to these goals; (c) sac-
rificing time, effort, and pleasures so that the demands of the discipline are
met; and (d) striving for goals that go beyond personal desires and needs and
instead benefit other people and society as a whole.

This sense of satisfaction with the "good work" stems, almost entirely,
from my reverence for social psychology. As an undergraduate, I displayed a
dilettante's interest in many topics before I strayed—by accident—into a
course in social psychology. As the professor (Dr. Russell D. Clark III)
moved through the material I was thrilled that my own ruminations were
shared by a vibrant, expressive community of scholars. Their view contrasted
so sharply with conventional wisdom, for many people seem to return time
and again to explanations of human behavior that stress personality and
predilections as causes of behavior. My sixth-grade teacher, for example, was
certain that each one of her pupil's destiny was already determined at the age
of twelve, that our aptitudes and temperaments had already set us on our
life's course. My mother and grandmother, both astrologists, similarly believed that one's outcomes depended little on the actions of others, more
on the predetermined course set by the planets. Yet, here was a field that
confirmed that other interpersonal and not intrapsychic events shape people's outcomes. I became a professor because that is what social psychologists become. Yet I am a social psychologist first, and a professor second.

But this detached fascination is complemented by a belief that social psychology offers important insights into many of the problems of living in the
modern world: collective violence, cults, destructive obedience, intergroup
conflict, mental illness, overcrowding, pollution, and prejudice are all examples. In my studies of prosocial behavior (actions that benefit others rather

than the self), my students and I find that morality is as much a quality of social groups as a characteristic of isolated individuals. Studies of our social identity model explain how individualistic qualities—traits, beliefs, skills, and so on— are melded in the self-concept with qualities that spring from membership in groups, including families, cliques, work groups, neighborhoods, tribes, cities, countries, and regions. And my studies of the functions of groups—the rewards that people gain by joining with others in a group—explain why sociality is so common, particularly in times of challenge and stress. This general approach to understanding how individualistic needs are coordinated with, and in many ways met by, membership in groups forms the theoretical basis for my analyses of how group psychotherapy can be improved.

My belief that my discipline offers partial answers to key questions facing society and its citizenry shapes not only the subjects I study but also the way I teach. When they first begin their studies, my students often think like intuitive personality psychologists: they focus exclusively on personal qualities and attributes, such as personalities, attitudes, and inclinations, and downplay the importance of the connection between the individual and the group. Eventually, though, I convince my students to join me in the analysis of social psychological issues, thus broadening their perspective and understanding of human behavior.

A science can only flourish if its findings can be taught to new generations of students. Thus I feel that my greatest contribution to the field may be the Ph.D. students who have earned their degree with me and have gone on to become professors themselves. I also hope that my undergraduate students, although unwilling to dedicate themselves exclusively to the study of social psychology, may nonetheless carry with them from my classes an appreciation of the significance of these processes.

When I was a neophyte teacher my enthusiasm for the field led me to expect my students to become "junior social psychologists." If a social psychology edition of Trivial Pursuit existed, I would have used it as my final exam. With experience, however, I learned that gaining an overall view of the field was more important than learning all the specific details of the field. To help them achieve this goal, I use my knowledge of group dynamics to de-center my classrooms with small group discussions, online study groups, collaborative learning activities, and team methods.

My faith in the value of the social psychological perspective has also prompted me to support the discipline itself, not just through teaching and research, but by contributing to its infrastructure: its professional societies, its journals, and its conferences. I have organized scientific meetings and institutes devoted to group topics, served on editorial boards, defended my discipline's perspective when serving on scientific review panels, and been active in seeking to unify the social psychological analysis of groups with the use of groups in applied settings. My concern that studies of groups were being overlooked by editors prompted me to found a journal devoted entirely to the study of groups, with the intent of providing an outlet for empirical studies of groups from a variety of disciplines.

Moving forward, I hope to continue my work examining interpersonal relations and groups; to understand how they function, sustain us when we are traumatized, and help us accomplish tasks that would overwhelm us as individuals. I admit that social psychology cannot fully explain modern society—humans' cruelties and their inhumanity, its wars and prejudices, and its horrible television programming—but I would like to think that my work in understanding social phenomena will lead to answers that will inform how we will meet the challenges that lie ahead. I am convinced that with time, research, and conceptual development, my colleagues and I will contribute in substantial ways to the improvement of the quality of life both here and abroad.

FORENSIC PSYCHOLOGY

Psychologists are also making their presence known in the courtroom. They are frequently called in to give expert testimony during criminal trials, and many work with interdisciplinary teams to prepare multimedia support for lawyers who are attempting to describe complex material to juries. Movies such as *Silence of the Lambs* and events like the O. J. Simpson trial have led to an increase in popularity of applying psychological principles to the courtroom.

While some forensic psychologists deal more specifically with the clinical aspects of victims or defendants by counseling victims, evaluating their ability to testify in court or to assess a defendant's mental competence to stand trial, others work as consultants to law enforcement officials. These consultants may be involved in creating profiles in order to apprehend criminals (such as the behavioral science unit of the FBI), or they may use their clinical and research skills in the evaluation of potential jurors. These latter psychologists evaluate the verbal and nonverbal behavior of individuals in attempts to predict pro- and anti-criminal sentiment. One such forensic psychologist, Stanley Brodsky, Ph.D., from the University of Alabama, clarifies this important role in the criminal and legal system in the following conversation.

~~~

Courtroom Psychology
Stanley Brodsky

One popular but incorrect image of forensic psychologists is that we cleverly piece together subtle clues about serial killers that lead us with certainty to a profile that tells us, for example, that the killer is a well-groomed young man who keeps his shirt always buttoned to the top, who tortures neighborhood cats, and who lives with an aged aunt who is unaware of the photos of mutilated victims taped to the inside of his closet door. Yet, the actual work of psychologists with the law is every bit as much a detective story.

Take the psychologist's work with somebody who pleads not guilty by reason of insanity to a murder charge. The legal issue typically is whether the defendant was mentally disordered and did not know right from wrong at the moment the trigger was pulled. The work of the forensic psychologist is to look at information before and after that moment in order to make a professional judgment of what was going on at the moment of the killing. To do that, we assemble and interpret prior and subsequent mental illness histories, examinations, records, and behaviors.

We take it as a professional and intellectual challenge to piece together such fragmented information. In the same sense, making assessments of emotional damage in civil lawsuits and helping to select juries is what crossword puzzles, long-distance running, and fly-fishing are to many other people. It calls for preparation, patience, and the practical application of what has been learned in psychology classes and experiences after school.

The greatest challenges that we face are to put forensic work together with good research foundations and to stay impartial. Practicing psychologists of all kind often find themselves relying on intuitive judgments, which is not an altogether bad thing. However, intuition can get in the way of relying on the scientific literature.

When I testify in court about my findings, good attorneys ask how I know what I know. When I am at my best, my answers describe standardized procedures, research applications, and how practicing psychologists are always developing and testing hypotheses. Staying impartial is sometimes tough. Attorneys are part of the fierce adversarial process of defeating their opponents (and, when cases go to trial, at least one side always loses).

Attorneys wheedle, hint, and occasionally plead that I tilt my opinions just a little bit toward what they want. In response, I ask them if they are trying to put words into my mouth, and that usually serves as a conversation stopper.

Working as a forensic psychologist with lawyers and the courts can be heady and exhilarating. After a trial or deposition that has gone well, I often feel like skipping and dancing down the street. As the same time, it is demanding work with a lot at stake. It is not for the meek or the shy.

THE PSYCHOLOGY OF PEACE

Today a growing number of psychologists worldwide identify themselves as peace psychologists. Through his writings and efforts in this burgeoning field of study, Professor Dan Christie, Ph.D., from Ohio State University, has helped capture the main intellectual currents that are growing and defining this emerging subdiscipline. He has provided workshops for a new graduate program in peace psychology at the University of Florence in Italy and remains dedicated to research and practice that bears on the prevention and mitigation of violence between individuals, group, and nations.

Peace Psychology
Daniel J. Christie

Some people choose a career by considering how well their abilities match various jobs, but my story sounds more like the accident theory of vocational choice. As an undergraduate at Ohio University, I changed my major several times, but ultimately majored in psychology primarily because I enjoyed psychology courses more than other courses. When the Psychology Department at Ohio University offered me early admission to graduate school—a program that allowed me to take graduate courses for undergraduate and graduate credit—the prospect of pursuing a Ph.D. in psychology seemed like a good idea. Developmental psychology was most appealing to me partly because I had children and I saw the study of developmental psychology as a way to deepen my understanding of them while integrating my academic and personal life.

When I completed the Ph.D. in 1975, the job market was tight and because I had a family to support, I took the first offer that came my way. I wasn't very savvy and didn't realize I would get a number of other offers for interviews. But I was reasonably satisfied to begin my career in a position that emphasized teaching at a regional campus of the Ohio State University, thinking I would quickly move on to other positions that would allow me to do more research. Now, thirty years later, and in the same position, I can say with certainty that my interest in teaching grew over the years, far more than I expected. My efforts were rewarded at Ohio State through teaching awards. I found it natural to care about students and their academic and personal development, and also felt I was making a difference in their lives.

I was content to publish journal articles in a wide range of areas (psychophysiology, developmental psychology, educational psychology) at the expected rate, which was about one refereed publication per year. But around the time I received tenure in the early 1980s, my research with children was consistently indicating that their main concerns had nothing to do with my research agenda. In interviews with children, they talked about their worries and fears about the prospect of nuclear war. I soon began to pursue research and teaching assignments that helped me better understand the dynamics of the nuclear arms race and, more broadly, the psychological causes of adversarial political relationships. I became very interested in methods that could manage conflicting views constructively in order to prevent the outbreak of violence.

Fortunately, just as my passion was growing and my career was gaining meaning and direction, professional organizations that focused on the threat of nuclear war were gathering momentum. Organizations such as the International Society of Political Psychology, Society for the Psychological Study of Social Issues, and Psychologists for Social Responsibility supported my growing interests in international relations and the prevention of nuclear war. The resources of Ohio State also were helpful, allowing me to affiliate with the Mershon Center (for the study of international security) and to live abroad for two years while I taught and conducted research in the Malaysian Cooperative Program, a program designed to address the disparities in wealth and health among the ethnic groups of Malaysia. More recently, the university accommodated my interest in teaching on Semester at Sea, a shipboard educational experience that circumnavigates the globe. All these experiences over the past twenty years contributed to my professional development and to the enthusiasm and insights I was able to bring back and share with my students.

In 1990, when members of the American Psychological Association formed a new division, Peace Psychology, I found my home in the profession. Some years later I served as president of the division and later as president of Psychologists for Social Responsibility. I have also reviewed a reference book on peace psychology that will be published in the United

Kingdom. In 2001 I edited a volume with Richard Wagner (editor of the journal *Peace and Conflict: Journal of Peace Psychology*) and Deborah Winter on *Peace, Conflict, and Violence: Peace Psychology for the 21st Century*. The book has helped capture the main intellectual currents that define this emerging field, and I feel extraordinarily fortunate to be part of that effort. It's clear to me that the rest of my life will be devoted to the many challenges ahead in maintaining a peaceful world.

CHAPTER 4

The Ins and Outs
of Graduate School

GRADUATE SCHOOL: A LONG
BUT PRODUCTIVE PROCESS

The stories within this book are from individuals who have achieved many successes in their chosen area of psychology. Hard-working and creative, these professionals used their doctoral degrees to access careers that gave them much lifelong satisfaction. They became professors, researchers, consultants, practitioners, and writers. Through their vocations they were able to influence the next generations of students in their research, teaching, and clinical work and life directions. And through their stories they may influence you. It now becomes important for you, the reader, to see for yourself whether graduate school in psychology, or the pursuit of any advanced professional degree, is indeed the right choice for you.

The first thing to ask yourself, of course, is, "Why go to graduate school at all?" The satisfactions derived from a career in psychology have been initially answered, at least, through the many affirmative "voices" heard within the pages of this book. The successful teachers, scholars, and clinicians who have offered their personal stories throughout this book seem to agree that it was the challenge and excitement of learning, as well as the sharing of those pursuits with intellectually curious colleagues, that enticed them into the field. Indeed, the passion of pursuing an interest and the ensuing process that doing so entails, along with the rewards it brings, is what makes one's career an arduous but exciting journey!

GRADUATE PROGRAMS VERSUS CAREER GOALS

In thinking about life after college and deciding upon the right direction, you need to ask yourself: "What type of career do I want?" and "What types of graduate programs are available to meet my career goals?" (Nietzel, Bernstein, Kramer, & Milich, 2003). If your primary interest is in research or if you want to receive significant training as a teacher, the Ph.D. program is probably your best option. However, you must take into account that pursuing a Ph.D. takes time—time needed to focus intently on specific areas. The years required to achieve a doctoral degree will be well spent in developing personal interests as well as learning the skills necessary to communicate them effectively. Through these years, your developing research skills and your experiences in teaching and theoretical studies will allow you to become a competent professional-in-the-making: they will provide you with a solid foundation for your future.

If your interest lies primarily in clinical work, a variety of options are available. Many students seem to think that to do clinical work, they must enter a Ph.D. program in clinical psychology. In fact, approximately three times as many students who become clinicians earn master's degrees in psychology compared to those who have obtained the doctoral degree (Morgan & Korschgen, 2001). Many students considering clinical Ph.D. programs could probably meet their educational and employment needs with a master's degree in clinical psychology or in other programs that offer the training that can lead to effective careers in the mental health professions, such as social work, school counseling, expressive therapies, or marriage and family therapy programs. Also, at the doctoral level, Psy.D. programs may provide more direct clinical training through their emphasis on applied experiences and therapeutic and diagnostic skills, rather than focusing on research.

INCREASING ADVANTAGES OF MASTER'S DEGREES

Recent trends in our health care system have led to increased enrollment in health maintenance organizations (HMOs). Through their cost-savings methods, they often focus on hiring master's-level professionals, rather than individuals who have received their doctorates in clinical psychology. In fact, many believe that master's-level professionals from psychology and related fields will enjoy many opportunities for direct service roles, whereas doctoral-level clinical psychologists will tend to take on more administrative, supervisory, grant-writing, consulting, and program evaluation roles in the future.

Thus, the M.A. in clinical or counseling psychology may be a more marketable degree than it has been in the past. Further, what is seen as the biggest drawback to the M.A. degree—the need for continual supervision from a licensed Ph.D. psychologist—may be changing. Many states are passing legislation that allows M.A.-level psychologists and other master's-level clinicians to be independently licensed (as licensed professional counselors), which allows third-party reimbursements and professional certification to deliver services. This new trend in providing mental health care gives many master's-level practitioners almost equal standing in the eyes of the public. Thus, before investing all your efforts in applying to doctoral programs in clinical psychology, you may want to explore the clinical job opportunities available to professionals trained at the master's level. This is especially true if you are committed to a full-time direct-care career, with little interest in spending a considerable amount of your graduate education on research-related activities.

THE PASSION OF A DOCTORAL EDUCATION

Enrollment in graduate school should be prompted by passion. It should be encouraged by a love of learning, not just because it will lead to a particular job. The end goal truly is not always about the money, for attending graduate school means delaying career-related jobs and possibly substantial monetary earnings for many years. Obtaining the Ph.D. or Psy.D. takes considerable time, effort, frustrating moments, and much hard work. The successful graduate student must have strong motivation and clear focus. You need to please many professors and related staff by their initiative, intelligence, and understanding of departmental policies. In the end, you must really want to be in a particular program to reach your goal of being called "doctor."

With this perspective, it helps to have a good idea of a career direction, even though you may follow different paths in pursuing your degree and eventual job. Areas of specialty are increasingly important, especially in today's environment, where expertise in certain areas can provide many rewarding options. Also important is researching various graduate schools. From the beginning attempt to match your ideas with graduate programs and individual professors who may share interests. Remember, when you enter graduate school, you are taking on a huge commitment to pursue a life goal; your results may be better if you have a good idea of what to expect. Thus, one worthwhile venture is to scan topical books and current journals in your areas of interest. Another is to attend conferences in your region to learn what schools, departments, and individuals are engaged in the type of clinical work or research that you would like to be involved in.

OBTAINING FEEDBACK

If you are truly considering graduate school, or even after obtaining a master's degree are thinking of pursuing a doctorate degree, it becomes imperative for you to discuss your ideas with your current faculty or other professionals in the field. Also, do not hesitate to e-mail faculty or graduate students in other programs for advice. Most are accessible and can suggest areas of study or encourage you to read their research. Even if you receive only brief answers, the feedback will be important.

Asking questions will help you to narrow your choices and may increase your opportunities for admission, especially if the professors you contact become interested in working with you. And don't feel that it is enough just to get into a graduate program! This is your life and career direction, so plant the seeds of your desires early and learn enough about possible programs and mentors to satisfy most of your questions about your future years in school. Even if you aren't admitted into your "first choice" program or that "name" school, you can still contact professors from these programs and with their advice or encouragement possibly extend their research into your setting.

A CONTINUOUS CYCLE WITH A POSITIVE ENDING

At this point, it must seem that getting ahead never ends. If you did "everything right" in high school, you were able to get into a "selective" college; and now if you do "everything right" again, you might get into a "selective" graduate program. Of course, this upward spiral never ends, for even in graduate school, your involvement in research and clinical activities, your experiences with faculty members, and your opportunities to teach or assist in teaching courses are what get you that first "selective" job. And it still takes much effort to become successful in your independent work, whether as a researcher, teacher, or clinician. Yet surely you will agree with those who have offered their stories here that the journey to an advanced degree is well worth the time to make the rest of one's life full and fruitful.

DOING YOUR HOMEWORK

In your investigative pursuit of graduate programs try to discover at least two faculty members whose interests are similar to your own. In this manner, if one professor does not assist you as you envisioned or simply cannot give you the time or support you require, you'll have a chance of success with another faculty member, one who may help you develop your interests within his or her research or clinical team.

Also crucial is accessing information about the community of graduate students within a particular program you are pursuing. Again, it is easy to communicate through e-mail to find out about their interests and lifestyles. Your feeling comfortable in a new environment will help you focus more easily on studying and working in areas important to you. Remember, you are investing considerable time and money over a two-to-five or even six-year period, and you do want a successful conclusion to your efforts. Much of that success comes from being part of learning communities of students who may very well be a part of your future. These peers can also help you in gaining financial support, comfortable housing, and other ways that will make your years more productive.

THE REALITIES OF APPLYING
TO GRADUATE SCHOOL

Even if you have taken all the right steps in preparing for graduate school entrance, be realistic about pursuing doctoral programs. Only so many slots are open per year, and there are always many outstanding students, just like you, applying to these schools. As you may guess, even highly qualified applicants are often rejected.

As with applications to undergraduate school, you really do need to apply to a range of programs, understanding that some may reject you. However, many programs are available to eager students, so expand your interests. Numerous programs exist outside traditional clinical ones. You may want to enlarge your scope by investigating doctoral training in school or counseling psychology. Also consider departments with industrial-organizational, applied developmental, or basic experimental focuses. These programs often have more opportunities for scholarships and assistantships that lessen the financial burden of postgraduate work. With this broadened base of possibilities you are more likely to find a right fit for your unique interests and personality.

Of course, similar to applying to undergraduate colleges or universities, you increase your chances of getting into selective graduate schools by earning excellent grades and a high score on the Graduate Record Exam (GRE). However, it is also important to take courses outside of psychology, such as higher-level math and science courses. In addition, it is always helpful to demonstrate your interest in psychology by attending professional meetings, assisting in research, volunteering for experiments, and doing relevant work. Talk to professors and graduate students at your current school; they need to know you personally to better write future letters of recommendation that will go beyond a general description of your assets for continuing your education. It is also a good idea to investigate funding sources for your future research ideas, as this demonstrates your planning abilities as well as your independent-mindedness.

THE UNIQUENESS OF A GRADUATE SCHOOL EXPERIENCE

Attending graduate or any type of professional school is certainly a unique experience. It requires intense study and focus, huge sacrifices, and delayed gratification. And there is usually much soul searching and many ups and downs along the way! At first there is bound to be an overwhelming feeling of unmet needs, chronic worry, little sleep, second guessing, and just bewilderment.

For many new students, graduate school is unlike anything else they have encountered. They are not necessarily convinced that all courses are relevant, and they are certain they cannot possibly recall all the information being taught to them or read everything required of them. Demands are never-ending, and nothing is ever completely right! They also face numerous milestones along the way—lengthy term papers, comprehensive exams, clinical experiences, research projects, a master's thesis, and a doctoral dissertation.

Where to set priorities and how to manage time when so much is expected? It becomes a good reminder that these questions have been asked by many generations of graduate students. Also remember that most graduate students do manage to complete all requirements and do eventually obtain their desired goals.

Another important point to consider is the need for self-discipline. Just when students need the most structure and support in their lives, they quickly discover that the graduate environment is often unstructured and requires much independent work and disciplined work habits. Vague time constraints are the norm after the second or third year, when less classes are required and more time is devoted to research topics and clinical practica, internships, or other psychology-related experiences. At this stage of graduate study, the preparation for one's future is usually governed by one's interest and priorities with few built-in milestones or rewards to support progress.

THE RESEARCH GRIND

When involved in research programs, students initially spend most of their time in the library in anticipation of developing sound ideas and implementing them. Reading journals, discussing ideas with colleagues, and revising drafts of proposals become core activities of the day. It becomes crucial at this point to be very familiar with any specialized field you are entering. You must appreciate and understand the experiments and data accumulated on your topic of interest, and you must stay current to show professors and colleagues that your research ideas are relevant and up-to-date with the literature. Possibly up to half of your time during the beginning is spent reading. Although this is typical and what you might have expected, staying motivated within the developing relationships in graduate school may lead to many distractions. Of course, you also may feel overwhelmed by the amount of reading you need to have covered and just want to give up (but this usually does not happen).

HOW TO STAY MOTIVATED

Once past the initial shock of graduate school, you begin to realize that you indeed belong to this group of scholars, theorists, and research-oriented clinicians. However, there comes a time, particularly in the middle years, when maintaining a positive attitude and staying motivated becomes a challenge. The daily grind, tests that continually press your insecurity buttons, and the anxiety created by knowing that your twenties are quickly passing you by, that you are not having as much fun as your peers who ventured directly into the workforce, all try your patience. Although these stresses may be normal for a graduate student, they undermine your motivation and initiative.

When immersed in such negative thoughts and feelings, you really need to find a sympathetic ear—another graduate student perhaps, or your advisor or a friend or relative outside of school who can understand the rigors of the graduate school experience. Besides venting your concerns, specify your stumbling blocks and take the time to identify small, concrete steps you can take to improve the situation. To stay focused on your studies and work, it often helps to have outside activities to force you to manage your time more effectively and to remain busy and directed each day. Having regular meetings with your advisor or other faculty members, attending seminars (even outside of your department), and taking the time to enjoy extracurricular activities such as sports or music can actually help you maintain a regular schedule.

Also, try to be realistic about what you can accomplish. Feeling stuck in graduate school is really not a pleasant experience. Give yourself positive feedback for tasks you do complete, instead of focusing on your failures. Setting small goals is always a good idea. And it works even better if built-in rewards are used, in addition to having another student review your progress. For example, I remember sending another graduate student "stars" for weekly achievements on her dissertation just to get her started; then her own inertia took over and she was able to work independently and productively. Before we agreed on this simple reinforcement system, she was simply feeling frustrated and demoralized about completing all her doctoral work requirements.

Of course, teaming with a group of individuals who are focused on similar work is an ideal situation. Ideas can be exchanged, immediate feedback can be given, support becomes an integral part of the experience, and the joy of learning can really be experienced. Also, more ways are discovered to break down ideas and workloads into manageable parts. Everyone becomes instrumental to each other's success. And every task completed gets everyone closer to finishing the program with more completed activities on their resumes.

FINAL STEPS TO COMPLETION

Even though the middle years in graduate school seem an eternity, they are only the stepping blocks to what most people consider the hardest part of completing a Ph.D. program, that is, completing an original project and writing and defending a dissertation topic. This stage of graduate school is a culmination of everything learned up to that point in time: using one's skills to discover and research a thesis topic, to undertake the methods required to conduct the study, to write the thesis (usually in four long parts: introduction, research methods, results, and discussion), and to defend its validity to a group of professors (and sometimes other students) is actually a remarkable process. Truly, this is a unique though anxiety-provoking experience. It is not for the meek and frustrated, as many ABD (all-but-dissertation) individuals can relate in their abbreviated journeys. However, if you have a good advisor and a support network of faculty interested in your research topic, as well as friends, this final step in your formal education is likely to meet with much success and satisfaction.

FINDING THE "RIGHT" ADVISOR

Finding the "right" advisor will help you immeasurably in completing a thesis or dissertation. Ideally, finding a good match began with the application process. Perhaps identifying amicable faculty led you to apply to a specific graduate program. If this did not occur, begin looking for good working relationships with professors the minute you enter your program. Whatever the "right" traits are, a supportive advisor and mentor shares work and pleasure interests and has a similar or complementary temperament or personality style. He or she is doing high-level, quality work and remains interested in presenting research at conferences and in journals. In my own case, I was fortunate, probably because I was a returning student (later twenties), to find several faculty members who shared common passions, both psychologically related and recreationally (tennis, racquetball, and Sunday brunches).

Beginning this process when applying for graduate school is important. Search on the internet. Faculty bios on websites can offer good overviews and tell how the faculty members fit into their particular departments. Also, read research journals. These articles can give you many ideas about possible research paths during the next several years. This process is so important in enabling you to take personal control of your future. Such exploration allows you to strengthen your position as well as broaden your choices. Finally, attend regional or national conventions where these potential professors may be presenting talks or their graduate student teams are presenting their research at poster sessions. Such firsthand experience will offer you not only a closeup of the research that may have piqued your interest but also a picture of how these professors or graduate students relate as people and how their personal interests are integrated into their workdays.

Talking to older graduate students can also be a rich source of information. You may gain valuable feedback about their relationships with the faculty, learn about the pitfalls they have encountered in completing their work, and discover how successful they have been in getting their research results into conference presentations or published in journals. It is certainly well worth the time to speak with graduate students directly or over the internet, or to ask more general questions through the psychology graduate student association, which can be found through the APA website (www .apa.org).

QUESTIONS TO ASK

When you contact faculty and graduate students from prospective schools, you may want to focus on specific questions. These inquiries may center on interpersonal relationships, such as how available are the faculty, how open are they to your or other outside ideas, how independent do they expect you to be, and what financial support might be available to members of the research team. This latter question may be especially important in your pursuing funds for your graduate education. Although having a built-in graduate assistantship job certainly helps, it is equally important to pursue your own interests and not get too side-tracked by short-term financial gain. Remember, you are giving up much of your freedom and potential full-time work salary over the next few years to pursue your unique interests.

Another question is whether a particular faculty member is new to the program or is a first-time grant winner who is building a new research team. Although there are advantages to having more directional choices within a new group (you may have more freedom and influence), you may find yourself isolated, without the knowledge that experienced graduate students can offer. Discussing these issues with potential faculty members and fellow students within that program can provide you with clearer views of what you will actually be doing during your next few years.

Finding a principle advisor means finding a person who will, in most cases, be your mentor and role model during your graduate education. This person should be a source of technical assistance, as well as part of your personal support system. A mentor can help you find the resources you need to make life more comfortable during these years, such as living arrangements, financial support, and equipment to ensure your maximum productivity. He or she can introduce you to relevant people in your field, encourage your research interests, and provide direction for your thesis or dissertation. Most important, your mentor can help you determine career options and assist you when you are ready to find that first job.

Once you identify one or more potential advisors, try to get to know them through brief introductions at conventions or by asking questions about your areas of interest. Also ask about possible research or teaching assistantships and what ongoing research projects are available. Of course, you need to familiarize yourself with their work. Read their published papers or hear them speak at conventions. Also learn about the activities of their students. If you have the opportunity, make an appointment during their office hours to elaborate on your questions and to offer any specialized services you may be good at, whether proofreading and editing or computer-related expertise.

PRACTICAL CONSIDERATIONS

As suggested by the many personal stories in this book, especially from those contributors who discussed their mentors, the experiences students have with their advisors and other faculty will be unique. Whereas some students prefer structure and direction and frequent contact, others are more independent and are more productive on their own. Also, some students may need direct contact but are not assertive enough to obtain it, whereas others may be too imposing. Personality styles also direct the kinds of feedback preferred—whether the student needs "random" ideas or very directed feedback; whether the preferred work is individual or in groups; whether the involved work is on established research projects or a newly designed efforts; or whether the student feels more comfortable working in the same area as the advisor or doing something in collaboration with an outside faculty.

The chances are, however, that you will be involved with many professors and mentors throughout your graduate experience. No one individual can provide you with all the information you will need during these years. Having more than one mentor or advisor is common and also very useful. Mentors and advisors may come from other departments or outside the university environment. For example, you may find yourself with a research assistantship in another setting, especially if you are connected to a medical school, or in a clinical placement in the community. Of course, you may become closer to people your own age, like senior graduate students, rather than faculty, or you may continue to have contact with your undergraduate mentors.

You may want to change advisors over time, especially if your advisor has changed focus or may no longer be easily accessible (remember, advisors are invested in their own lives and careers and have other students and families to please). You will also be undergoing many transitions during this time and may prefer a more encouraging advisor around you, whereas before you may have wanted more critical feedback. Also, you may find that your advisor, though a good clinician, lacks the technical background to guide you through your dissertation. The most important thing is to be politely assertive in defense of your own needs.

BEYOND GRADUATION

Once you have obtained your formal education, you are faced with the ultimate question, "What next?" You soon realize that all the years spent in school are leading to this next stage in your life. And you soon understand that what you have learned are many skills, the keys, that will open many doors. Whether you are refining your dissertation for defense or applying to internships or postdocs, no doubt much anxiety and excitement accompany your thoughts and dreams. You are certainly confronted with taking that next step and wondering just how your new life as a psychologist will turn out. Of course, many self-doubts may enter your musings as you compare your resumes with those of other students, but most certainly you will find a niche, whether as a professional clinician, researcher, or teacher. Such uncertainties are common among new psychologists. Remember, you will have much accumulated knowledge by this time and many desirable skills, even as a student. You will eventually find a job, though likely it will not be your ultimate job or even one that will last more than a few years.

In reporting these bound-to-be fears in an issue of the online graduate student newspaper of APA (*gradPSYCH*), reporter Jamie Chamberlain asked several early career and seasoned psychologists what worked for them during their educational process and what advice they had to offer future students (Chamberlain, 2004).

One of the first psychologists approached emphasized the importance of becoming known early in your career. This psychologist, Shane Lopez, Ph.D., of the University of Kansas noted that you need to let your "personality and passion" drive your early professional identity. Likewise, Robert Sternberg, Ph.D., of Yale emphasized the need to "be true to yourself." He noted the enormity of outside pressures but espoused that personal success comes from being happy with what you are doing and finding meaning in the venture.

Well-known psychologist Philip Zimbardo, Ph.D., of Stanford focused on the need to become a top-notch teacher, especially in courses such as introductory psychology and statistics, to set yourself apart from fellow graduates. He also mentioned that researchers should work in collaboration and on larger projects, which receive most grant funding, as opposed to individual investigations. And private practitioner Robyn Landow, Ph.D., offered the important advice of remaining connected to former colleagues, since you never know what you will be doing in the future and they may be involved in interesting work you may like to explore. Likewise, Sharon Berry, Ph.D., a children's hospital clinician, stressed the need to take care of yourself through training and career development, even leaving a workplace you perceive as detrimental, for many jobs remain out there to investigate.

Also important is the need to stay connected to the discipline of psychology once you have graduated. Many psychologists cited in this book stress the need to give back to the profession and to the public at large. They accomplished this through local, state, or national work in psychology. Past president of APA Dorothy Cantor, Psy.D., for example, encourages psychologists to serve on committees and respond to legislators. Advocating for psychology is a lifelong profession, she reminds everyone, and many bills in Congress can be influenced by local activity.

Another former APA president, Diane Halpern, Ph.D., also stresses the notion that psychology is an interactive business and that it is important to continue networking throughout one's career. Finally, Norman Anderson, Ph.D., APA's chief executive officer, emphasizes the need to "work your butt off" once you have identified your passion and have obtained a job commensurate with that pursuit. He adds that you should not hesitate to offer what you have learned as a psychologist, because "you've had great training," and that in doing your job, you must remember to "have some fun."

KEEPING YOUR SANITY

You will have to believe people who espouse that finding a balance in graduate school and during your early professional career is extremely vital, but not always so easy to accomplish. You will often hear conflicting advice from your advisors, your fellow graduate students, and your family: some people will say that you should spend every waking hour working on completing your dissertation or finishing that latest project; others will say just relax, there is always work to be done. Most people, though, will acknowledge that even the most productive workaholic doesn't always achieve what he or she is after and that the workaholic lifestyle may be unhealthy or the goals totally unrealistic.

Thus, for your mental and physical health remain involved in outside activities. This caution is especially relevant if you are married or have responsibility for others, because you will then have to balance your priorities even more carefully. Graduate school and early career development indeed place much strain on relationships, so make sure you save time and energy for those people you care about.

One key in attempting to balance your life is to initiate a schedule that is fairly consistent. This regularity may mean that you will work only during the day hours and that evenings are devoted to other activities. Of course, you have to decide when you are most productive: Are you a morning person? Or are you more accomplished in the late afternoons? You may decide that long lunches are your way to unwind, or that exercising in the afternoon is best for you, and then it is off to work until late into the night. For some individuals, the weekend is the time to take care of oneself. For others, the weekend hours may be the only time they have for solitude, among all their other activities, to study or think without distractions.

Graduate students usually hit the doldrums around the end of the second or beginning of the third year, a time when they are attempting to complete their required coursework and focusing on a research topic, so they will find engaging in activities that are beyond the rigors of school useful and enjoyable. They usually return to familiar hobbies, such as music, crafts, physical training, or a subject outside psychology. These activities give pleasure and help remove the feeling that you are just drifting. At this stage, time away from school is important because the next stage of completing a dissertation can be very time consuming and focused, leaving little time for relationships and fun. Knowing that things will become more focused, you can warn friends and family so they don't add unnecessary pressure to your time commitments. Only after your dissertation and defense is completed can you return to normalcy—at least before your job search begins and the next stage of your life commences.

YOUR CURRICULUM VITAE

Your first job after graduate school, like all future jobs, is based on your academic and experiential history as described and integrated into your personal history. This history is usually summarized on your curriculum vitae (or CV), something you will be constantly revising throughout your working life. This resume tells who you are as a psychologist and, as the initial document potential schools or employers receive, can determine whether you will get an interview. Thus, it is crucial to make this historical outline as complete as possible.

Your resume can take many forms, but certain information needs to be organized to catch the reader's attention. Basic data, such as your name and contact information, need to be stated clearly. Your colleges, dates of graduation, and degrees earned should all be included, as well as any specialized training or licenses. Next, your completed research, teaching, or clinical experiences need to be explained in detail. Finally, presentations, publications, organizational memberships, and awards must be listed clearly. Simple, straightforward, and possibly tailored to fit a particular job or position—these characteristics are key to ensuring that someone will pay attention to your resume.

Job hunting is always competitive. Thus, compose your CV with much care and forethought. As Tara Kuther, Ph.D., from Western Connecticut State suggested in an interview for the graduate student online newsletter, "A vitae that is formatted nicely, attractive, looks professional and presents your strengths really stands out to employers" (Dittmann, 2003). This emphasis means that a vitae—a CV—highlights your educational accomplishments as well as your experiences and work duties. It is sufficiently detailed to cover all your history, not just provide a brief overview, as a one-page resume usually does. Your potential employers need to know as much about you as possible, and you do not need to shortchange yourself at this point.

To maximize your CV, develop a cover letter that highlights your acquired skills, in particularly when you are applying for a specialized job, such as child clinician or researcher for a specific population or within a certain laboratory. Incorporating a cover letter allows you to call attention to future research ideas, clinical experiences, or specified courses you have taken that may overlap the job requirements and are not found on the CV. This customized letter should emphasize your strengths and tell why, in your opinion, you are the right choice for the position. Finally, ask a colleague or friend to edit your letter and CV to discover potentially confusing formatting or awkward phrasing. Ask for feedback on clarity and content. Through the cover letter and CV you make a personal statement and convey your history; and both need accuracy and clarity to accentuate your potential. The extra effort to "get it right" is worth the effort.

CONSIDERING THAT FIRST JOB

Seeking that first job comes with much trepidation. Am I really ready to step out into the "real" world? Do I really want to continue a life in academia? Do I need more training to become a professional caretaker? Should I take that first offer? Am I prepared for interviews?

Throughout my own career, I have had the opportunity to support and advise many students on their initial voyages into job interviews. Their anxiety and insecurities were paramount. Their uncertainty about what to expect was real. My being there after their rejection was always difficult for me, but very important and necessary.

The challenge of finding jobs after graduate school is exhilarating as well as exasperating. For most students, a lack of perspective leaves them uncertain of their next step into the working world. They have vague ideas about their future, but they know they need a job, and they really do want to move on and test themselves outside of their academic or clinical home. It is indeed time to leave the nest.

So what to do? First, become aware of what is realistically available. Read the classifieds from APA's monthly newsletter (*APA Monitor*) and from the *Chronicle of Higher Education*, which lists many teaching and counseling jobs among smaller colleges and universities. Look at your departmental bulletin board for postgraduate research or postdoctoral clinical training. Also, look outside of psychology. Many medical schools, such as Johns Hopkins in Baltimore, have enormous research grants and are looking for clinical researchers to lead various teams in population and intervention studies. Especially around Washington, D.C., there are numerous private research companies who are subsidized by NIH and NIMH to coordinate their research ideas and are looking for new, talented psychologists to develop surveys, analyze data, and write papers for presentation and publication. For clinicians, go to state, county, and local professional organizations' websites to discover job opportunities. Complete their applications. Once your name is on a state or county list and you have met the minimum qualifications, you will be sent notifications for possible interviews at different facilities.

Most importantly, make a plan. This is your first undertaking, and you have the knowledge and the energy to utilize your talents and prove yourself in a new arena. So, decide what you want. Do you see yourself as a teacher, clinician, or researcher? Is teaching at a small college with mostly undergraduates more desirable than working in a large research-based university that has many graduate programs? Do you want to live in a large city, or do you prefer living away from the traffic? Do you want to continue on an academic path on a college campus, or would your skills be better used in a medical school or in a private organization? Is moving back home or closer to family important?

Let us examine some recent advertisements from the *Monitor* and *Chronicle* to see whether they might be enticing to you:

Psychologist (experienced) needed to perform assessments and therapy in Fetal Alcohol Syndrome. and Drug Exposure clinics.

The National Institute of Child Health and Human Development (NICHD) is seeking a behavioral scientist for research planning, development, and administration.

Department of Neurology offering two-year post-doctoral Fellowship in clinical neuropsychology.

Teaching position for psychologist at community college; starting salary from $40–57,000. Master's degree required.

Hospital has vacancy for Ph.D. psychologist to perform assessments, assist in treatment plan development, and provide and supervise individual, group, and family therapy.

University is searching for an assistant professor who specializes in adult development. In addition to being a dedicated teacher, the applicant should have a record of publication and the research skills to supervise master's theses.

Psychologist is needed to provide school psychology services with youth diagnosed with developmental disabilities and autism.

Faculty needed to teach in areas of counseling, abnormal, and one specialty area, such as forensics.

Tenure-track psychology position to teach History and Systems, General Psychology, and senior-level Advanced Topics in Social and Industrial/Organizational.

As you can see by these job descriptions, the skills of a student who has successfully completed a graduate psychology program are vast. And they continue growing! Whether you teach, conduct research, or do clinical work, you will find yourself immersed in new ideas and gaining new skills, especially over the next five years after your formal education has concluded. You will acquire more knowledge. During these years, you will be developing your unique style as a teacher or clinician, attending workshops and conventions, and just growing in confidence in yourself and in your skills. You will also be a supervisor, and these skills too will add to your competence in daily interactions. Formal and informal continuing education remains a requirement for licensure and insurance purposes, whether you find yourself in private practice or in an organizational environment, such as a hospital or in the military.

Thus, finding that first job is just one more step in the process of your personal development. But you do need to view it as more than just a job. It is truly a transitional step into higher-level responsibilities. During your job search, you not only want to be valued as a knowledgeable resource but also to have at your disposable the support and wisdom of more experienced teachers, researchers, and clinicians. This will help you to expand your knowledge base and will ensure your continued growth. For instance, if you view yourself as a researcher, make sure the faculty opening you are seeking allows you enough time to continue your ideas and can provide you support—if not financial, then equipment and students—to carry out your needs. A clinician also needs constant input from others to discuss treatment strategies, to spend time reviewing case histories, and to receive continuing feedback about his or her own therapeutic style.

THE INTERVIEW PROCESS

In most cases securing graduate school admissions, internship opportunities, or employment requires a personal interview. This is usually a requirement for final selection. First of all, if you are invited for an interview, you are in a relatively small pool of select applicants, and regardless of the outcome you should feel proud of yourself. Don't forget that there are many qualified applicants looking for a job at the very same time! However, you do want to optimize the impact of your interview, both in the information you gather and the impression you make. To do this requires preparation and practice, and so you should take several steps prior to your interview. These may include: (1) becoming familiar with the program and the people you will be seeing; (2) reading published articles by the faculty for teaching and research positions, and theoretical papers for specialized clinical work environments; (3) preparing to speak at length about your own research or about specific clinical topics you know well; and (4) planning in advance what questions may be asked to you and what questions you want to ask the faculty or staff.

When having your site visit, take the opportunity to talk with current graduate students in the program or new faculty. During clinical visits, you may want to focus on the client population and get a feel of the neighborhood. You may also want to talk with professionals other than psychologists to gain an appreciation of how psychologists are viewed.

Ask questions similar to those you asked of prospective schools and faculty when you were applying to graduate school. Topics emphasizing mentoring, collegial relationships, and strengths and vision of the program are all relevant areas to discuss. Of course, what you say to other students or professionals may likely be shared with those individuals in charge of hiring, so avoid saying critical things about what you have seen or contradicting yourself about your career views.

Your interview style and especially your presentation need to be polished, thoughtful, and interpersonally comfortable. Both teaching and clinical placements require many unpredictable interactions, and the hiring faculty are viewing you as someone who is potentially representing them in public. Although you may feel understandably nervous during these visits with students and faculty, remember that they need to examine your fit into their environment. In the process, they will present you with many people to meet and situations to confront. Thus, your interviewers have to maximize their time with you. At the same time, you want to gain as much information as you can to determine whether you truly want to be in this setting for an indeterminate time.

So again, preparing and practicing for these interviews are paramount to a successful conclusion. Be prepared to make notes concerning the questions you have, the answers you obtain, and the knowledge you have gained from reading articles about the setting or particular faculty. Go to websites and know the history of the setting, whether it be a college, university, or hospital. Gain an understanding and appreciation of where you are and how your personality style, work ethic, and ideas will complement the program. And don't rely on your memory! The interview process can be stressful, so reviewing notes before a personal interview can be quite comforting.

Practicing interview situations is also key to making a poised presentation of yourself. Rehearse with friends and colleagues through role-playing exercises. Get faculty to ask you tough questions about your goals, research results, or therapeutic style. Be prepared for anything personal (e.g., how do you fit into your family of origin?) or general (e.g., can you describe in detail a five-year research project that would likely be funded?).

Also, make presentations with power-point slides before you begin your interview. You can usually ask professors to allow you to present during one of their classes, or you can present at student organization meetings. You can also call on local mental health clinics that may be looking for presenters at their weekly staff meetings. If you can arrange to be videotaped, all the better for critiquing your performance. The more you take these steps seriously, the better prepared you will be for any event or possibility thrown your way at these job interviews. Given the importance of the interview in the final selection process, you want to do everything you can to ensure success. Good Luck!

CHAPTER 5

Pioneers in Psychology

PAST LEADERS IN PSYCHOLOGY

This chapter speaks to the breadth and depth of psychology. The past fifty years have brought forth talented and creative researchers, teachers, and mentors who have contributed greatly to the establishment of psychology as an esteemed profession. By reading this chapter you will discover the history of several of these special individuals and hear their "voices," thereby becoming well informed about their contributions to the field and seeing how their expanding ideas have enlarged our lives. They all have been exemplary in their work habits and in sharing themselves with the people who surround them. This chapter is a tribute to their times and to their continuing energy to make psychology a better-informed science.

James N. Butcher received a Ph.D. in clinical psychology at the University of North Carolina–Chapel Hill in 1964 and was awarded an honorary doctorate (Doctor Honoris Causa) from the Free University of Brussels, 1990. He has maintained an active research program in the areas of personality assessment, abnormal psychology, cross-cultural personality factors, and computer-based personality assessment. In addition, he has published 50 books and more than 175 articles in the area of personality assessment, abnormal psychology, and psychotherapy. One of his best-known areas has been his contribution as a member of the University of Minnesota Press's MMPI Consultative Committee, which actively engaged in a large-scale project to revise and restandardize the MMPI.

Dr. Butcher, who is now professor emeritus from the University of Minnesota, founded the Symposium on Recent Developments in the Use of the MMPI in 1965 to promote and disseminate research information on the

MMPI, and he has organized this conference series for nearly forty years. He also founded the International Conference on Personality Assessment, a program devoted to facilitating international research on personality assessment. He has been actively involved in developing and organizing disaster response programs for dealing with human problems following airline disasters. Through this work he established a model crisis intervention disaster response for the Minneapolis–St. Paul Airport and organized and supervised psychological services following two recent airline disasters: Northwest Flight 255 and Aloha Airlines' Maui accidents.

Personal Assessment and the MMPI
James N. Butcher

My career in psychology has taken me to many faraway places and provided me the opportunity to collaborate with many psychologists and psychiatrists in other countries. One of my research areas in psychology involves cross-cultural personality and clinical assessment—an area I have been asked to teach in over twenty-five countries and to collaborate on research projects in many more. My interest in cross-cultural psychology emerged many years before I became a psychologist.

I became an orphan at an early age and had the unusual circumstance of growing up in a family without adults, only myself and three other minor children to take care of ourselves. This set of unfortunate circumstances instilled in us a sense of independence and clear motivation to succeed in life. On my path to adulthood, I enlisted in the U.S. Army at age seventeen and served as an infantry soldier during the Korean War. During this war, which was a United Nations operation, I had the occasion to serve alongside soldiers from other countries such as South Korea, Ethiopia, Colombia, and Turkey under conditions of high duress. At that time, I gained both a respect for and a great interest in the personality makeup of people from highly different cultures—an interest that has persisted throughout my working life as a university professor.

My career in psychology has taken a number of simultaneous paths—university teaching and working with graduate students on projects has been particularly rewarding. I have had the opportunity to supervise fifty-five doctoral dissertations during my career and worked with many graduate students who went on to outstanding professional careers. Areas of interest that I have pursued as a professor include research in abnormal psychology, exploring the application of computer-based personality assessment, personnel selection (particularly air crew personality screening), and crisis intervention and disaster management. For example, following several commercial air crashes I was asked to establish psychological services for employees who were experiencing adjustment problems after the trauma.

Each of these career directions has been professionally rewarding for me. However, as I look back over my forty plus years as a college professor, I find my international involvements to be especially rewarding—and continuing even after my retirement from the University of Minnesota. Even today, rather than passively sitting out my retirement years, I find myself involved in international research activity and packing my suitcases and PowerPoint presentations and heading out for faraway places.

Harry C. Triandis, Ph.D., who is professor emeritus from the University of Illinois at Urbana-Champaign, is considered the father of cross-cultural psychology. Over the years, he has authored numerous books, including *Attitudes and Attitude Change* (1971), which became a citation classic. His *Analysis of Subjective Culture* (1972) included extensive empirical work done in Greece with Vasso Vassilious and resulted in an honorary degree from the University of Athens in 1987. Recent books have included *Culture and Social Behavior* (1994) and *Individualism and Collectivism* (1995). He was also general editor for the six-volume *Handbook of Cross-Cultural Psychology*.

Dr. Triandis's research over the years focused on the ways people in different societies define their self-concept. His work led to training programs on how minority group members adjust to society. His interest and dedication through the years was acknowledged by the APA with a lifetime achievement award. Other awards include becoming a fellow of the American Association for the Advancement of Science and being a Distinguished Fulbright Professor to India.

Cross-cultural Psychology
Harry C. Triandis

When I was in high school I observed that people from different cultures behaved differently. I wanted to find out why this was the case. Studying psychology gave me that chance to find out. It was very gratifying to me that I was able to develop theories that provided an explanation of cultural differences and make systematic observations that confirmed these theories. It was also most satisfying to see my books translated into several other languages.

For my research I had to work with colleagues from many cultures and I found very satisfying getting into their shoes and figuring out what made them tick. I learned a lot from them. Many times I collected some data with their help and then analyzed the information and showed them my interpretation of what we got, and they had a different way of looking at the results. I generally had to agree with the way they looked at these results.

Thus the work was satisfying both because it provided an intellectual explanation and because it gave me a chance to relate to people from all over the world. It was especially gratifying that I could collect data in Australia, Costa Rica, Germany, France, Hong Kong, Japan, India, Indonesia, Korea, The Netherlands, Greece, and the United States, as well as among racial and Latino minorities in the United States.

Another source of satisfaction was having good students, who became successful research psychologists in their own right. It was also satisfying to be invited to teach and give lectures in different countries. I taught in China, India, New Zealand, and Singapore, as well as in the United States at the Universities of California, Cornell, and Hawaii (many times). I lectured in about sixty countries, ranging from Argentina and Australia to Nigeria and the Netherlands to Venezuela. I made friends around the world, and that is perhaps the most satisfying part of my career.

Born in New York August 2, 1938 (James Bruce Wheelwright, later adopted), J. Bruce Overmier received a B.A. degree in chemistry from Kenyon College, an M.A. degree from Bowling Green State University in general psychology, and a Ph.D. degree in experimental psychology at University of Pennsylvania in 1965. Now professor emeritus from the University of Minnesota, he has been professor of psychology (graduate faculties of psychology, neuroscience, psychoneuroimmunology, and cognitive science) and was executive officer (1973–1978; 1981–1983) and director (1983–1989) of the Center for Research in Learning, Perception, and Cognition (now, Center for Cognitive Science). In 1990 he received an honorary doctor of science degree from Kenyon College, and in 2000 he was recognized as one of the Outstanding Scholars of the Twentieth Century. He also held appointments as Professor II at the University of Bergen (Norway) since 1992 and has held term teaching appointments at the University of Hawaii (United States), Kenyon College (United States), University of Bergen (Norway), Kansei Gakuin University (Japan), and University of Seville (Spain), as well as visiting research appointments to the University of Newcastle (Australia).

Dr. Overmier's research spans specialties of learning, memory, stress, and psychosomatic disorders and their biological substrates. This research has been carried out with a variety of species of laboratory animals (fish, birds, and mammals), as well as with human client volunteers (with Down's syndrome, Korsakoff's syndrome, or Alzheimer's disease). The laboratory animals serve as models for various forms of human dysfunction and the development of therapies (e.g., "learned helplessness" first reported and named by Overmier & Seligman, 1967, and popularized by Seligman as a model for depression, although it may be a better model for post-traumatic stress syndrome). Dr. Overmier has authored some 200 refereed research articles, book chapters, and books in his specialties.

Psychobiology and Cognitive Science
J. Bruce Overmier

Science has intrigued me since I started reading science fiction early in high school. But during my college studies of the core sciences, I was distracted first by a girlfriend and then by two lectures in psychology she took me to on her campus during my last year. These lectures were on (1) the "executive monkey" phenomenon wherein stress induced fatal ulcers, and (2) the POWs during the Korean War wherein reasonably healthy young men POWs sometimes "gave up," pulled a blanket over their heads, and were dead the next morning. The message I took away from this was that the "mind" could kill you!

This seemed so important that I abandoned my B.A. major (chemistry) and applied to graduate school in psychology. There I had the good fortune to work with marvelous, flexible mentors, first John R. Schuck, who stimulated my research in issues of controlling uncertainty, and then Richard L. Solomon, who taught me about "fear," defense, and coping. In many ways, these early experiences have continued to shape my researches.

I became interested in the consequences of uncontrolled trauma on later learning, leading to the initial demonstration of "learned helplessness"—and likely not unrelated to either the issue of uncertainty or those POWs that Edgar A. Schein had interviewed. Later, my asking the question (sensible in the 1960–1970s) of whether different fears were differentiable by the individual led me into my researches on differential outcomes of responses and how "expectancies" of these outcomes can guide behaviors; this of course was a complete break with traditional Thorndikian psychology of learning in which reinforcers were viewed merely as catalysts of learning and not learned about.

But I never quite forgot about those executive monkeys, and in the 1980s returned to study how helplessness-inducing operations modulated ulcer formation—in animals. I add "in animals" because I also became interested in the whole broader concept of animal models of human dysfunction—the various kinds of models, the structure of models, their functions in science, and importantly their usefulness in advancing our understanding—even treatments—of human dysfunctions.

My interest today in fostering the study of animals in basic psychological research focusing on mechanisms of brain and behavior stands on all those past experiences taken together. It stands in spite of the almost faddish trends of contemporary cognitive psychology, its "neuroimaging" phrenology, and emphasis on "higher-order" cognition that seems at times to ignore that basic bio-behavioral mechanisms likely underlie it all. Of course, there is room for both, need for both, and they will someday reinforce each other.

I have never regretted my change of field some fifty years ago. I have worked hard for psychology as a scientist and in the organizations that support psychological science, committing thousands of hours to its management. I did—and do—so because psychology needs to be organized to compete with the other sciences that are well organized for the funding so critical to both students and scholars. Psychology has been good to me, and I turn now to fostering its development in the international arena.

John H. Flavell, Ph.D., who is professor of psychology at Stanford University, has spent many years pursuing developmental research on children's knowledge about the mind. His brilliant book on Jean Piaget (1962) opened American psychology to the power of the structural descriptive approach to children's thinking; his theoretical essays have continued to make him the seminal thinker in the field. He has completed groundbreaking research in four different domains: children's memory, metacognitive development, role taking, and communication skills.

Dr. Flavell has taught and conducted research at Stanford for over thirty years. He has been Honored with APAs Distinguished Scientific Contribution Award, and has been elected to the National Academy of Science, both considerable achievements for this internationally recognized developmental psychologist. Considered the founder of social cognitive development in psychology, he was one of the first psychologists to study the ways in which children think.

Studying the Child's Mind
John H. Flavell

As I look back over my life and my career as a developmental psychologist, I am struck by two facts. First, many things that happened later couldn't have been predicted from things that happened earlier: there were a number of unexpected, often fortuitous zigs and zags. Second, both life and career have proven to be pretty happy and successful despite the fact that I lack a number of talents.

As to unpredictability and fortuitous happenings, consider the following examples. I was good in chemistry in high school and planned to major in it in college. In college, I was terrible at it (because it was real chemistry, not the dumbed-down version we were served in high school) and so I tried biology. Not talented at that either I switched to psychology, which seemed a lot easier.

In my senior year, I applied to grad school in clinical psychology at Harvard and Clark Universities. I was accepted at both but only Clark offered any financial support. Believing that grad students need to eat as well as learn, I decided to go to Clark. It proved to be a fateful and very fortunate choice. Clark professor Heinz Werner, an inspiring developmental theorist, sparked an interest in developmental psychology that could not have happened in the Harvard of those days—or most anyplace else, for that matter.

After getting my Ph.D. at Clark I got a job at the University of Rochester as an assistant professor in the clinical program. By pure happenstance, the person teaching developmental courses in the department had just left and, as the only available professor with some background in the area, I was elected—once more an unforeseeable nudge toward a career in that field. There were other nudges: a planned book on developmental theorists ended up being a book about only one theorist—Jean Piaget. I never imagined that this book would be so widely read and inspire great interest in Piaget everywhere, but it did (I also didn't realize until well into the book that Piaget and I shared the same birthday—unforeseen predestination again?).

Similarly, an initial interest in Vygotskyian inner speech led unexpectedly to an interest in rehearsal and other memory strategies and hence to metamemory and metacognition. Concentrating in developmental rather than clinical by this time, I moved from Rochester to the University of Minnesota's Institute of Child Development. There were great students and colleagues at the Institute and consequently my research flourished during that time. I spent the year 1969–70 at the Center for Advanced Study in the Behavioral Sciences. It just happened that a Fellow that year was Eleanor Maccoby. Thanks largely to her initiative, I was subsequently invited to join the faculty at Stanford. We moved to Stanford in 1996 and lived happily ever after.

And what about my life outside of psychology? Well, take my marriage to Ellie Flavell, the love of my life after more than fifty years together. And how did we meet? A blind date, of course. I sometimes think that my whole life has been one big Blind Date. Moral: some ability is clearly nice, but dumb luck is even better.

Speaking of ability, I'm not going to claim that it was all dumb luck, of course. The truth is that I am pretty good at some things but decidedly poor or mediocre at many others. The many others include tennis, golf, bridge, piano, typing, fixing anything, household finances, statistics, and anything else mathematical or logical, computers, finding weaknesses in my own or other people's research, and remembering anything for more than five minutes. I really don't consider myself as having one of those high g, laser-like minds. On the positive side, I do think a lot (pencil and pad in hand while sitting on the beach—that sort of thing), and I sometimes have good intuitions about possible developables. I am also a good pool player, the fruits of a misspent adolescence.

So there may be a moral here, too: You don't have to be good at everything; you would like to be good at a few things. And sometimes just a few things will get you somewhere—especially if you also have dumb luck.

M. Brewster Smith, Ph.D., professor emeritus, University of California at Santa Cruz, has been considered the elder statesman of social psychology. A book of his essays covers McCarthyism as well as the Bush administration's "War on Terrorism" (Smith, 2003). As a young social psychologist in the early 1950s, Dr. Smith served as an expert witness, testifying against school segregation in a case before the federal appeals court in Richmond—one of four upon which the Supreme Court based its 1954 ruling against segregation in *Brown v. Board of Education*.

Dr. Smith received a Gold Medal Award from the American Psychological Foundation for his Lifetime Contributions to the Public Interest. Over the years, he conducted groundbreaking work on the ways in which people's opinions are influenced by their strategies for coping with the world, with their social relations, and with their inner conflicts. He has also drawn on psychological research to suggest ways to reduce threats of nuclear war. In a speech at his former college, he suggested that "psychology should be involved in social action. An understanding of human psychology can have a great impact on social policies." When contacting him about his life he made the following comments:

Social Psychology and the Public Interest
M. Brewster Smith

I came into psychology as an undergraduate at Reed College in the mid-1930s for reasons that are not uncommon. I was troubled by what Erik

Erikson later labeled as an identity crisis that I hoped psychology would help me understand, and I had a wonderful psychology professor, "Monte" Griffith. Another reason that affected the directions I took in psychology was the fact that it somehow linked the perspectives of the two fields I had previously thought of majoring in: biology and history. (There was a senior girl, a psych major, who also mattered.)

I had marvelous professors and mentors at Stanford and Harvard before I got drafted in World War II who got me involved in serious research as an undergraduate and graduate student. I had published work in animal psychology and human experimental psychology with my Stanford mentors before the war, and in the army I had the challenge to function as a psychologist in test development while I was an enlisted man, then as an applied social psychologist in important survey research overseas after I became an officer. In finishing my degree in social psychology at Harvard after the war, I had the luck of coming into the academic job market when it was at its height of postwar expansion.

This launching started me committed to a view of psychology that was both humanistic and scientific (I don't accept the supposed conflict between science and humanism) and also relevant to contemporary social issues. It also schooled me in interdisciplinary relations.

In research, the high point of my career later was my study, with an able graduate student, of the experience and performance of the first Peace Corps group to serve overseas—as teachers in Ghana. Members of this group and I are still lifelong friends. In public policy, I'm especially proud of my role as an expert witness for the NAACP at the federal court in Richmond in one of the cases feeding into *Brown v. Board of Education*, the Supreme Court case that ended legally enforced racial school segregation over fifty years ago, though it did not end segregation.

Psychology has been an exciting field to participate in—changing a great deal from emphases on behaviorism, then on variants of psychoanalysis, then on cognitive psychology. The changes reflect the complexities of the field and its embeddings in the society and culture of the time. I think there have been great gains in knowledge and method, but I do not expect psychology to come to rest. It will remain exciting and it will continue to change.

Leonard Berkowitz, Ph.D., Vilas Research Professor Emeritus, University of Wisconsin–Madison, grew up in New York City and attended New York schools through his undergraduate years. After service in the U.S. Air Force, he received his Ph.D. from the University of Michigan in 1951 and has been on the faculty of the University of Wisconsin–Madison since 1955, although he has also held visiting appointments at Stanford University, the Center for Advanced Study in the Behavioral Sciences, Oxford, Cornell, and Cambridge Universities, and the University of Western Australia, as well as at the University of Mannheim.

Professor Berkowitz was one of the pioneers in the experimental study of altruism and helping. His studies in this area, starting in the early 1960s, focused mostly on the conditions affecting the extent to which individuals will work in behalf of others requiring their assistance. This laboratory research led to a public opinion survey investigation of what Berkowitz termed the "traditional socially responsible personality," a personal disposition to act in socially approved ways in behalf of the community.

Dr. Berkowitz is best known, however, for his research into situational influences on aggressive behavior, based mostly on laboratory experiments but also on field interviews with violent offenders in the United States and Britain. Relatively early in his experimental program, around 1960, he conducted laboratory studies of the aggression-enhancing consequences of watching violent actions on the TV or movie screen.

In the past two decades Dr. Berkowitz turned his attention to emotional feelings, with special emphasis on anger. He has extended this approach even further by applying it to hate crimes and other instances of attacks on members of racial and ethnic minorities. The author of about 170 articles and books, mostly concerned with aggression, he was also the editor of the well-known social psychology series Advances in Experimental Social Psychology from its inception in 1964 to his retirement from this post in 1989.

Altruism and Aggressive Behavior
Leonard Berkowitz

Several times now friends of mine who regards themselves as "humanistically" inclined have told me why they object to the "scientific" approach to the study of human behavior. They believe strongly that an insistence on methodological rigor, precise terminology, and statistical analyses is devoid of mystery and wonder. These "scientific" investigations, they say, make human beings less interesting. I strongly disagree. We cannot separate scientific research from the sense of wonder and a strong interest in the mysteries of human conduct. Good science is often driven by curiosity.

But of course, scientific investigations should not be propelled merely by the desire to see what people will do under such-and-such circumstances.

They are usually most fruitful when they are guided by a theoretical formulation offering a fairly specific prediction as to how persons are likely to react to a particular circumstance. Several of my most gratifying times as a research psychologist have arisen from the results of experiments in which my theoretical analyses have been confirmed.

One notable example is provided by my initial study of the so-called weapons effect. Convinced of the important role played by associations in influencing aggressive reactions, I was fairly sure that people already disposed to aggression for one or another reason would experience a stronger urge to aggression than they otherwise would have had merely as the result of seeing a nearby weapon. The sight of a gun would stimulate a stronger aggressive response than otherwise would have occurred. I was not surprised, but was indeed pleased, when the Berkowitz and LePage (1967) experiment confirmed this expectation. Other investigations prompted by this associationistic perspective were also especially gratifying. I have long proposed that scapegoats for displaced aggression (such as Jews or African Americans) are apt to be attacked by angry persons because (among other reasons) these minorities possess stimulus qualities that evoke strong aggressive impulses from those who are aggressively inclined. Extending this line of thought, I also believed that the aggressive urge elicited by viewing violent behavior on the movie or TV screen was especially likely to be subsequently directed at those persons who have particular stimulus qualities: namely, a fairly strong association with a previous frustration and/or with aggressive behavior generally. Again, a series of experiments, from my laboratory and elsewhere, have upheld this prediction.

I think it's fair to say the pleasure I felt on these occasions had two related sources. It of course was gratifying to think my theoretical analyses could be correct. But in addition, and related to this, I was also pleased to find that here too, in the study of human behavior as in other fields of research, much of the universe was orderly and understandable.

Wayne H. Holtzman, Ph.D., professor emeritus, University of Texas at Austin, has devoted over fifty years to personality assessment. His well-known creation of the Holtzman inkblot test (1961) was an attempt to overcome the deficiencies of the original Rorschach inkblots. He served many years as president of the Hogg Foundation for Mental Health and several years as dean of the College of Education at the University of Texas. He also conducted extensive collaborative research in Mexico, in areas of child rearing, and as a naval officer in World War II developed interests in coping behaviors and reactions to stress.

Inkblots to Executive Leadership
Wayne Holtzman

What do you want to be when you grow up? Some people always seem to know the answer to that question, but few never veer from that course. Many seem to muddle through without a clue. At age twelve, I received a chemistry set for Christmas and was struck with inspiration. "I want to be a chemist!" Fortunately, as the years progressed, I was flexible enough to adjust to a variety of circumstances and to take advantage of unforeseen opportunities that proved to be fulfilling.

What you think you might want to do when you are in high school or even when you have finished your undergraduate studies is often very different from where you end up. Chance factors and unexpected opportunities play a bigger role than most people realize. It is important to recognize and seize an opportunity when it arises.

When I was in high school in the late 1930s, psychology was not part of the curriculum. I enjoyed the natural sciences, especially chemistry, mathematics, and physics, and did well in most academic subjects. Northwestern University offered me a scholarship, and I decided to major in chemistry. On the eve of World War II, it also seemed prudent to join the naval ROTC at Northwestern. Besides, I had been a sea scout and really liked the idea of becoming a naval officer. The bombing of Pearl Harbor settled it. I eagerly set off to focus on naval science and tactics while completing my chemistry major in a perfunctory manner. Out of curiosity I elected to take an introductory course in psychology. I found the topics easy to learn, but the teacher was boring and it never occurred to me that I might want to become a psychologist.

After graduating and being commissioned as an ensign in February 1944, I was ordered to join the U.S.S. *Iowa* in the Pacific as an anti-aircraft gunnery officer. Serving with the Third and Fifth Fleets in Pacific battles with the Japanese fleet meant long periods at sea, often with a fairly dull routine that was frequently broken by the excitement and terror of major battles. I had plenty of time to read books in the ship's library, including some dealing with psychiatry and psychology that I found particularly interesting. I had begun to wonder why men reacted so differently to battle stress. Some coped effectively while others panicked.

By the end of the war, I knew I didn't want to be a chemist even though I had majored in chemistry at Northwestern. I also realized that I didn't want to be a naval officer the rest of my life, especially when my July 1945 orders to Corpus Christi for flight training were abruptly cancelled because of the likely end of the war. After my ship returned to Seattle late in 1945, I was granted leave for a month to return home. My ship had sailed down to Long Beach while I was on leave. While returning to my ship in southern California, I dropped by Stanford University. The fall quarter at Stanford was over and few professors or students were still on campus. Fortunately, I found one professor of psychology still in his office, E. R. (Jack) Hilgard. We talked for about an hour, and I left Stanford feeling encouraged to consider graduate work in psychology. What impressed me most was that Hilgard also had majored in chemistry before moving on to psychology at Yale.

After discharge in June 1946 from the Great Lakes Naval Station near Chicago, I wandered into Psychology at Northwestern University and met with its chairman, Robert Seashore. When he learned that I had an engineering and science background, he offered me an assistantship on the spot. Seashore had earned a graduate degree in geology before continuing on in psychology, following in the footsteps of his father, who was a distinguished psychologist at the University of Iowa. Seashore had a small motor-skills laboratory and he needed a technician to maintain his equipment and build new apparatus, a job for which I was nominally qualified. In those days immediately after the war, the leading departments of psychology were hiring new professors and seeking graduate students from among the returning veterans. Course requirements for graduate degrees in psychology were fairly flexible and unstructured. It was easy for me to move quickly into advanced courses that I found interesting.

While serving as a lab assistant, I took on other responsibilities. I assisted other graduate students with their statistics and thesis typing. I also spent one night a week assisting A. C. Van Dusen with his industrial counseling center in downtown Chicago. A special project I enjoyed was helping Donald Lindsley build a portable, shielded room for his EEG and electromyography research. Additional support from the GI Bill made life as a student much easier, financially speaking.

As might be expected, my master's thesis in 1947 dealt with psychomotor research. I enjoyed my studies at Northwestern, but I kept my eye on Stanford as a first choice for continuing graduate work. I was overjoyed to receive a teaching fellowship at Stanford under Hilgard. My fiancée successfully applied to Stanford for a graduate scholarship in music education. After a wedding in Aberdeen, South Dakota, we were off to California on our honeymoon in our 1936 Ford with all our worldly goods.

Like many war veterans in graduate school then, I was in a hurry to finish my doctoral requirements so that I could begin a professional career.

Clinical psychology was still in its formative stages and represented an attractive option, but the Veterans Administration program would take too long. My purposes were better served by taking part-time work in the student counseling center, followed by a year's fellowship in neuropsychiatry for two days a week at the Stanford Medical School. My background in mathematics led me to choose mathematical statistics as an elected minor. Although viewed as a strange combination by some of my friends, it proved to be useful later in getting my first job at a good university.

During that universally anxious period of job searching while finishing my doctoral dissertation, Hilgard urged me to consider an offer to visit the University of Texas, where there was one opening in psychology. The Department at Texas had only eight faculty members. Half of the faculty under Karl Dallenbach, who had recently moved there from a distinguished career at Cornell, wanted someone to teach statistics and experimental design. The other half desperately wanted a newly trained clinical psychologist to raise their chances of getting approval of their graduate training program. When I flew down for an interview, I was impressed with the future prospects for psychology at Texas. The faculty liked my rather unique combination of a master's in experimental psychology at Northwestern and nominal training in clinical psychology, coupled with a strong minor in mathematical statistics at Stanford, because it suited their purposes perfectly.

The University of Texas grew rapidly, and I grew right along with it. The first year I taught six different courses, mostly graduate, and drove once a week to the School of Aviation Medicine in San Antonio, where I taught a graduate statistics course. My personal research flourished, and I received a large grant to study anxiety and stress in Air Force pilots.

A major opportunity for expanding my horizons arose after five years. The director of the Hogg Foundation for Mental Health, a private, grant-making foundation at the university, asked me to join the foundation full-time as associate director in charge of research. I was encouraged to continue my teaching of one course a semester in psychology. I was able to continue my personal research projects with outside funding as long as it didn't conflict with my new administrative responsibilities in the foundation. By 1955, I was well launched on a somewhat different career as a philanthropist in the field of mental health, one that allowed me to maintain my identity as a psychologist and an academic in a first-rate university—the best of both worlds.

The Hogg Foundation had sufficient income from a relatively large endowment to permit one-half of the annual income to be spent on grants to promising mental health research scientists throughout Texas. In the 1950s, few Texas investigators were well enough known to merit grants from such major sources as the National Science Foundation or the National Institute for Mental Health. Grants from the Hogg Foundation provided the initial support needed to conduct the pilot studies necessary for continuing support from national grant-makers, both federal and private. This philanthropic work proved most satisfying to me and helped me with my own long-range research plans.

A year's fellowship in 1962–63 at the Center for Advanced Studies in the Behavioral Sciences allowed me to complete my first book, *Inkblot Perception and Personality*. I was able also to expand my research on personality development by undertaking a major cross-cultural, longitudinal project involving 800 school children—400 in Austin, Texas, and 400 in Mexico City—in collaboration with my friend, Dr. Rogelio Diaz Guerrero, who was a noted Mexican psychologist.

After returning to the University of Texas in 1963, I was appointed chairman of a faculty committee to recommend a new dean for the university's College of Education. After a national search, to my complete surprise, all the members of the search committee urged the university president to appoint me as the new dean. Many years earlier, I had served as assistant chairman of the Psychology Department under Dallenbach in the College of Arts and Sciences. I had discovered then that I liked administrative work helping my colleagues progress with their careers, as long as I could continue some teaching and research. This new, unexpected opportunity to provide leadership for an important college proved sufficiently attractive that I accepted the appointment as dean of education for six years.

In this new position of leadership, I was able to convince thirty-six of my colleagues in key departments throughout the campus to join with me in supporting new developments in teaching and research within the expanding graduate programs of the college. We all were given appointments as professors of education in addition to our primary appointments as professors in other colleges of the university.

During my term as dean, I received job offers regularly from other universities. For both family and professional reasons, I preferred to remain at the University of Texas. The university was growing rapidly, and there was plenty of opportunity to grow with it. By the end of my term as dean of education, my long-time friend and mentor, Dr. Robert Sutherland, the founding director of the Hogg Foundation, convinced me that I should accept an appointment as his successor. Sutherland wanted to retire and the university system chancellor made me an offer I couldn't refuse.

I continued full time in this dual role as both president of the Hogg Foundation for Mental Health and Hogg Professor of Psychology and

Education until my retirement as president of the foundation in 1993. For ten years thereafter, I was urged by my successor to continue with the foundation on a half-time basis, year by year, until finally I retired completely.

Throughout my career, I was encouraged to become involved in both national and international activities. Among various professional boards and committees on which I served, one in particular led to a whole new set of international activities. In 1970, the American Psychological Association appointed me as one of two official, American representatives to the International Union of Scientific Psychology (later known as the International Union of Psychological Science). The union is an organization comprised of the leading national psychological associations throughout the world. Shortly thereafter I was asked if I would be willing to serve as secretary general for the union, a voluntary, unpaid position as the chief administrator for the union and its activities. Honored to be considered for this key post, I accepted the offer and served as secretary general for twelve years. I was then elected president of the union at its 23rd International Congress of Psychology in Mexico.

As I look back now on the sixty years that have passed since my graduation with a chemistry B.S. degree and commission as a naval officer, I see a number of places where opportunity knocked and I was flexible enough to change direction. At each decision point, embracing a new, unexpected opportunity took advantage of skills and experience that I had gained in previous activities.

Undergraduate training in mathematics and the physical sciences taught me certain technical skills and sharpened my analytical abilities. Leadership training and engineering courses related to the naval ROTC program helped me obtain part-time work while a graduate student. My military experiences served me well as I embarked on a major research program with the Air Force after moving to the University of Texas. The combination of clinical psychology and mathematical statistics, although highly unusual, was seen as especially attractive to the University of Texas, where I got my first professional job. Taking on administrative and philanthropic responsibilities while continuing my teaching and research greatly broadened my horizons, leading to additional opportunities. Research and professional activities in Latin America led to my appointment as secretary general and then president of the International Union of Psychological Science, as well as to other activities and much travel abroad.

My wife and I had an agreement that I would never travel abroad by myself. On many occasions I was able to take her and our sons along with me, enriching all our lives by travel to many countries. Throughout all the welcome but unanticipated career changes, my identity as a psychologist, an academic, and a research scientist remained intact. Retirement as a professor within a major university continues to provide many opportunities to be of service while also allowing more time with family, friends, and leisurely travel.

When I was asked to write this article, the emphasis was to be on the development of my career as a source of encouragement for others. My professional career has been only one part of my life. In my case, having a loving family and friends has been even more important. My wife, four sons and their wives, and ten grandchildren have contributed greatly to my vision of "What I want to be when I grow up."

CHAPTER 6

Meaningful Careers and Lessons Learned

CONCLUDING THOUGHTS AS A PSYCHOLOGIST

The following stories conclude this book. The writers are selected individuals who have served in roles as practitioners and professors. These individuals not only have made significant contributions to the field of psychology but have truly enjoyed their careers. Their words "sparkle" in relaying what they have experienced and what they have learned. From military and public health specialist, to department chairperson, and finally to professor and textbook writer, these psychologists share memorable moments of their lives and the turning points in their pursuits that made choosing psychology as a subject of study so important to them. They put 100 percent of their efforts into making their careers as psychologists meaningful. By sharing their life stories, they encourage readers to grab onto their enthusiasm and compassion to make their life's journey enriching and exciting. The first of these psychologists, Ernic Lenz, Ph.D., MPH (master's in public health), takes the reader on a fabulous journey based on his strong beliefs about giving back to society.

A Lifetime of Adventure and Appreciation
Ernest J. Lenz

One way to look back upon a career is to ask the question: Given a choice, would you do it over again? In my case, I surely would take the same path. Being a psychologist has given me wonderful opportunities to serve in public service venues and has added to a full life. I have had the opportunity to go back and work with the Special Forces unit of the military (my formative years as a psychologist), in addition to spending a year on Capitol Hill as a Congressional Fellow. Psychology even directed me into the Peace Corps as a volunteer at a later age. We are getting a little ahead of our story, so let's start at the beginning.

After high school and spending a not very successful year at college, I enlisted in the military. I became a paratrooper in the 82nd Airborne Division and enjoyed being an infantryman. With John F. Kennedy's interest in Special Forces Operations, especially guerrilla warfare, during the early 1960s a call went out for volunteers. Once in training, I was offered schooling as a medic. This turned out to be a rigorous but exciting course. In many ways, it set the pattern and direction for the rest of my life.

After finishing second in a class of sixty-five, it actually dawned on me that I could learn. I soon returned to college and received a B.S. in psychology from Loyola University of Chicago. I then applied for and received a direct commission as a Medical Service Corps officer and volunteered to return to Special Forces. During the next three years, I completed the Special Forces Officer course and the U.S. Army Ranger School. While assigned to the 8th Special Forces Group in Panama, I completed the Para Scuba/Para Rescue course. I loved being a team leader with a rescue detachment.

One day I happened to see in a bulletin that that the army needed candidates with field experience to train as clinical psychologists. Having really enjoyed my undergraduate work, I put in a request, thinking probably nothing would happen. A couple of weeks later, I received a phone call from a Col. Charles A. Thomas, the psychology consultant to the surgeon general of the army. Colonel Thomas was quite a person. He had served as a fighter pilot in World War II, in both the Royal Canadian Air Force and the U.S. Army Air Corps. After the war he obtained a Ph.D. from Penn State.

Two months later I began working on a Ph.D. in clinical psychology back at Loyola University of Chicago. Colonel Thomas told me: "Loyola said it usually takes five years, including the internship, to complete the Ph.D. Captain, you will do it in four and one-half years." And I did!

I was blessed at Loyola to have as my advisor Dr. William A. Hunt, a giant of American psychology. Bill had been the chief psychologist in the U.S. Navy during World War II. Among his many famous students are Dr. Joseph Mattarazzo and Dr. Ronald Walker. Bill Hunt was an absolutely superb mentor. He passed on to me his love of learning and his broad interest in many areas of psychology. He also instilled in me his love for public service.

My good fortune continued with my internship. In 1970 Colonel Robert S. Nichols was starting a community internship with an emphasis on both clinical skills and broad consultation services. Bob had just completed an additional master's degree in public health at Harvard University under the famed Dr. Gerald Caplan. Being located at Fort Ord, Monterrey, California, had many advantages. We had a large military population, numerous family members, and access to many superb civilian consultants in the San Francisco Bay area. In addition, we provided coverage for the Department of Defense Language School. We had outstanding supervision not only in our clinical work but also with our consulting efforts on leadership and the improvement of training.

For my first assignment after obtaining the Ph.D., I asked to return to a troop setting, where I could practice both clinical and consulting skills. I was assigned to the 101st Airborne Division, where I had the opportunity to set up a community model, work directly with the commanding general and his staff, and consult on management and leadership. On the weekend that we did not have to work, I ended up as team leader of the Division Free-Fall Parachute Demonstration Team, "The Screening Eagles."

Following this experience, I was on the faculty of two major U.S. Army schools, the Academy of Health Sciences at Fort Sam Houston, Texas, and the Organizational Effectiveness School back at Fort Ord, California. While at the Academy of Health Sciences, I held a concurrent appointment as assistant professor of health care at Baylor University, which had a co-operative training agreement with the U.S. Army. At the Organizational Effectiveness School, I had the opportunity to travel extensively to consult on leadership and management.

In 1981 I became the psychology consultant for the U.S. Army, Europe. For three years, in addition to maintaining a clinical practice at the U.S. Army hospital at Heidelberg, I traveled extensively to consult with various military formations. During this time, the opportunity presented itself for training in hostage negotiations and counter-terrorist measures. We then formed a re-action team to be ready to respond to the increasing terrorism in Europe.

Because I had field experience before becoming a psychologist, I was for-tunate in being the first army psychologist to be board selected to command a field hospital. Working with a 400-bed hospital with 398 soldiers assigned was a great honor and privilege. I was able to use everything I had ever learned about psychology in an applied setting.

Next came a tour as the chief of the Department of Psychology at Tripler Army Medical Center in Hawaii. Hawaii, with its diversity of cultures and its beauty, was an absolutely superb experience. I had the opportunity to con-tinue consulting. Since I had a sailboat in the military marina at Pearl Harbor, I met a lot of naval personnel. A destroyer squadron commander invited me to steam on one of his destroyers for a week to consult on leadership, management, and organizational development. The Security Police at Hickam Air Force Base were preparing for a worldwide competition on combat skills. They invited Dr. Ray Folen, a superb civilian psychologist at Tripler, and me to practice sport psychology with the team. The local Veterans Administration office worked closely with us. I had the opportunity to work with Bill Sautner of the VA and to set up the largest PTSD group in the Islands.

One day I received a call from the deputy commander of the John F. Kennedy Special Warfare Center at Fort Bragg, North Carolina. At the time, they were experiencing a very high attrition rate in Special Forces training. He requested that I come to Bragg to look at the situation. After several visits to Fort Bragg, the commanding general asked me to volunteer to become his chief psychologist. What wonderful opportunities and challenges came with that assignment! In many ways we followed in the tradition and standards set for us by psychologists who worked with Lieutenant Colonel Henry Murray, of TAT fame, in the Office of Strategic Services (OSS) in World War II.

Working with Special Forces officers, we set up a psychological testing and interviewing program during the twenty-one days our candidates underwent assessment and selection. The program greatly reduced the former attrition rate in both the enlisted and officer qualification courses. We also had a psychologist in attandence twenty-four hours a day during certain phases of the Survival course. All the instructors and interrogators assigned to the Survival course at Fort Bragg had to undergo psychology assessment prior to being accepted as instructors. We monitored their work very closely. We also consulted on high-stress courses, such as Combat Diver and Military Free-fall Parachuting, and we worked closely with the Army Research Institute (ARI) to establish research programs to validate our selection and training methods. On the academic side, we presented blocks of instruction on human behavior for the Civil Affairs Officer course and the Psychological Operations Officer course.

Three years passed rapidly. I knew that I did not want to go back to a hospital setting at that time. I really wanted to continue with an operational unit. The opportunity presented itself to volunteer to lead a Medical Assistance Training team in El Salvador during the civil war in the late 1980s. We set up field medical training programs, visited the combats zones to improve the evacuation of the wounded, helped set up civil action programs, and worked on improving the administration of both field and fixed hospitals. We had the opportunity to brief the U.S. ambassador, William Walker, and many general officers on the medical situation in El Salvador.

When the ceasefire was negotiated in February 1992, the guerrilla forces actually requested medical assistance, especially with public health issues, in areas they controlled. Our team was able to consult with them and offered assistance. As a psychologist, I was able to bring in consultants to write up a mental health plan to help deal with the aftermath of the conflict.

The El Salvador experience made me even more aware of the importance of national policy and international relations. I then applied for the APA Congressional Fellowship, spending a year on Capitol Hill assisting on mental health bills, to learn more about government operations and the legislative process. Once again good fortune smiled upon me. I found myself one of five APA Congressional Fellows for 1992–93. It was indeed an amazing year.

We started with an intensive orientation program, which lasted three weeks. We met members of Congress and attended lectures on government process, foreign relations, and domestic issues. Many of the lecturers were former Congress members or had served as U.S. ambassadors. We were invited to numerous receptions with members of Congress, Hill staffers, and other government officials. We learned to work with members of the Congressional Research Service. This organization, a part of the Library of Congress, prepares information papers for members of Congress and their staffs on every conceivable topic of interest.

Opportunity after opportunity presented itself for learning that marvelous year. I had the privilege of attending several of the Senate hearings on the prisoner-of-war–missing-in-action issue. It was awe-inspiring to watch Senators John McCain, Bob Smith, John Kerry, and others in action. On a daily basis I got to do legislative research, write drafts, meet constituents, and attend numerous briefings. Many of us got to accompany our House member back to the home district. During the year, we were provided numerous educational and social activities. Our holiday party was at the National Indoor Gardens. We attended events at the JFK Center for the Performing Arts and at numerous embassies and we did two special tours of the White House. The year passed too quickly.

It was now time for my final tour in the army. I returned to Triple Army Medical Center as chief of the Department of Psychology. Several years earlier when I was chief at Tripler, we had initiated the process to establish an internship program. By the time I returned, the internship program and three postdoctoral programs—neurophysiology, child psychology, and health—were already in place. Tripler is an ideal location for an internship. It is one of the best medical facilities in the Department of Defense. Tripler provides care for members of all branches of the armed services. In addition, patients from the U.S. Pacific Trust Territories are sent to Tripler for definitive diagnosis and care.

I always had an interest in public health. In fact, for me, mental health is public health. My interest in health, especially public health, had been intensified by my experience working on Capitol Hill. When I returned to Tripler, I enrolled in graduate courses in public health at the University of Hawaii. I had been planning on finishing the master's in public health when I retired from the army. Fate, however, dealt a cruel blow. In December 1994, my wife, Cathy, a retired U.S. Air Force nurse, passed away suddenly and unexpectedly. I was not sure what to do.

One morning I received a call from Vinnell Corporation. I had contacted them for information about their job opportunities. They had and still have a contract to train the Saudi Arabian National Guard. Part of that contract included the operation of an allied health sciences school. Because of my background as a psychologist and my experience teaching at service schools, I was hired to do faculty development. When I got to Saudi Arabia, however, they liked the way I wrote, so I was quickly promoted to chief of curriculum. Shortly thereafter I was promoted to program manager for the school.

The Kingdom of Saudi Arabia proved to be a good healing place for me. Working with a faculty from nine different nations proved to be challenging and interesting. I had to use everything I had learned as a psychologist over the years. Observing the intercultural variations between persons from many different nations was extremely interesting. Findings way to get them to collaborate was a challenge, but was fun for the most part.

Living and working in the Kingdom of Saudi Arabia proved to be a real adventure. I learned to love the beauty of the desert. I had the opportunity to visit the mountains around Abha near the Yemen boarder. There I got a lesson in history and humility. We walked on the Wadi Hali on a path that the camel trains have been using for over 4,000 years. I also got to visit the Nebatian tombs at Madin Sala. These were the same people who built the famous city of Petra in Jordan. On that same trip we stopped at the ruins of several of the railroad stations that Lawrence of Arabia and his forces attacked. We frequently had the opportunity to dive the Red Sea, one of the best dive locations on earth.

Another unique experience was an invitation from the minister of health of Kuwait to visit his country to see the efforts of the government in dealing with the extensive cases of post-traumatic stress disorder (PTSD) resulting from the Iraqi occupations. Words cannot begin to describe the atrocities were committed against the Kuwaitis. The emir had set up an extensive program for his people. We visited what was purported to be the largest library in the world devoted to the study of PTSD. We met with many Kuwaiti psychologists and other health workers. Everywhere we traveled, we saw indications that the Kuwaiti people will never forget the horrors of the Iraqi invasion and occupation.

After two years of working in the Kingdom and having reached my sixtieth birthday, I decided to head back to the States. My children and grandchildren wanted me home. Together with my older son, I bought a house in Austin, Texas. For the next three years, I would use this as a base as I traveled extensively and crewed on sailboats in the Bahamas, Hawaii, and Mexico. I attended Chapman School of Seamanship in Stewart, Florida, to learn navigation and seamanship. I almost took a job on an offshore oil rig delivery boat, but I decided to backpack in New Zealand instead. I got to New Zealand with the idea of staying about two or three weeks. I ended up liking the country and the people so well that I stayed three months. During that time, I also visited the Department of Psychology at the University of Otago in the city of Dunedin. New Zealand is one of the most beautiful and unique places in the world. I definitely want to go back.

It was a great retirement and I was enjoying it. More and more, however, I was thinking about how fortunate I had been in life. I decided maybe it was a good time to give back to life something for the many blessings that I have enjoyed. I was around when John F. Kennedy founded the Peace Corps. I always admired the idea and the ideals of the corps. So, I decided to go online to complete an application.

Also, since I had already begun a master's degree in public health, I decided to enter a Peace Corps program that required completion of an advanced degree prior to entering service. By this time, my friend and mentor Admiral Jerry Michael, had retired as dean emeritus of the School of Public Health of the University of Hawaii. He was living in the D.C. area and was adjunct professor at George Washington University. Since I missed Washington and since GW has such a good international health policy program, I decided to matriculate in their program. I am glad I did. Not only did I obtain an outstanding educational experience, but also Admiral Michael invited me to assist him in doing research on recruiting and retention in the Commissioned Corps of the U.S. Public Health Service.

I completed the program with the title Director of Research at the Foundation for the Advancement of Public Health. Finally, everything that I had previously learned as a psychologist could be put to use in this research. I enjoyed doing an extensive literature review on why men and women enter public service. We conducted focus groups. We met with the faculty of many of the schools of public health across the country. We had the opportunity to interact with many of the flag officers of the Commissioned Corps.

I was in Washington, D.C., on September 11, 2001, when the terrorists crashed into the Pentagon. I watched the smoke from the roof of my condo. Then and there I resolved to do my enlistment in the Peace Corps. I knew at age sixty-six, the army probably would not allow me back on active duty. I then decided the best thing I could do for my country was to accept the invitation I had received from the Peace Corps to serve in a Healthy Schools Project in Guatemala.

On January 12, 2003, thirty-nine of us gathered in Miami to process and to travel to Guatemala to begin fourteen weeks of training for the Peace Corps. On April 24, 2003, we took the Oath of Service from U.S. ambassador John Hamilton. Now, close to three years later, there are twenty-nine of us still here.

I was very fortunate in being assigned to Santiago Atitlán on the shores of Lake Atitlán. An awed Aldous Huxley called the lake "too much of a good thing." As *Lonely Planet* states: "Simply put, Lago de Atitlán is one of the world's most spectacular locales, period." The grinding poverty of many of the people is in sharp contract to the surrounding beauty.

As a psychologist, I really appreciated the behavioral objective of our Healthy Schools program. The major objective was to get the children to practice good health habits in school on a daily basis. For example, we strove for at least 80 percent of the students brushing their teeth after the school snack. If a school met the long list of behavioral objectives, it would be certified as a "Healthy School." This certification increased the school's prestige in the community. It also helped in obtaining international assistance. We trained the teachers in instructing health material. We started off by teaching ourselves. We also conducted workshops. Another dimension of our job was to work with the parents, local authorities, and nongovernment organizations (NGOs) to improve the sanitary conditions in each school.

In many ways, for someone trained in psychology, a tour in the Peace Corps becomes a living laboratory. You can see the results of schedules of reinforcement and what modeling and role play can accomplish. You finally get to use everything you learned in grad school!

Of all the wonderfully good things about being a psychologist, for me, the best part had been the opportunity to meet some really superb people. As Alfred Lord Tennyson points out in Ulysses, "I am part of all whom I have met." Many outstanding colleagues come to mind. Among them are Frank Rath, Morgan Banks, Cecil Harris, Gary Greenfield, Larry Lewis, Debra Dunivin, Jim Livingood, John Chin, Bob Nichols, and Ed Crandell, who went on to become the psychology consultant to the surgeon general of the army. Also among them is the man not only who became my friend and mentor but whose leadership by example earns him the title "our psychologist on Capitol Hill," Dr. Pat Deleon. Pat has done so much for so many. He deserves honors for being a truly great American. There are two other psychologists whose memory I would like to honor, Dr. Tim Jeffery and Dr. Fred Garland. Both were taken from us too early in life. Both contributed greatly to human welfare.

In summary, as I started out saying, I would gladly do it all over again. A career as a psychologist has been challenging and very rewarding. As my distinguished colleague Dr. David Mangelsdorff once said, "They were a lot of years, but they were good years." They were very good years, indeed.

The next story by Professor Steven Hinshaw, Ph.D., describes the influence of his familial experiences on his professional work.

Discovering Personal Meaning in Your Work
Stephen P. Hinshaw

Currently, I am the chair of the Psychology Department at the University of California, Berkeley, a position that gives me great pride. In fact, I am the first member of the clinical psychology area of the department (now called Clinical Science) to have held this title at Berkeley, which is a sign that clinical psychology—with its blending of basic science and applications to psychopathology, prevention, and intervention—is recognized as important in a "hard science" campus like ours. My goal is to give the reader a small idea of some of the work and contributions that I have made but, more important, to convey a larger sense of the origins of my choice of becoming a Ph.D. clinical psychologist and investigator of developmental psychopathology, the science that integrates study of normal and abnormal development across the life span.

In college (I attended Harvard in the 1970s), I was considering medical school. Yet I found myself increasingly immersed in and captivated by my volunteer work, which involved teaching a psychology course at a Massachusetts prison, working as a big brother for two boys in a housing project, and serving as a home therapist under the auspices of a local community mental health center treatment team. I came to realize that clinical psychology could provide me with an education in research methodology as well as clinical intervention skills, without the rote learning of medical school.

After graduating with an interdisciplinary major, I took three years away from school to work in the field, coordinating a small school program for children and adolescents who could not be housed in the Boston public schools and directing a residential summer camp in New Hampshire for children with developmental disabilities. The research and clinical skills I learned propelled me into graduate school in clinical psychology at UCLA, where I also minored in physiological psychology (now called behavioral neuroscience) and quantitative psychology. These diverse fields of learning gave me tools for some of my current work in directing research grants with complex data analyses and doing studies in psychopharmacology (i.e., studying the effects of medication, often in combination with psychosocial treatments, on children with attentional and behavioral disorders). My doctoral dissertation involved a series of treatment studies on children with the then-new diagnostic category of attention-deficit disorder, in which I contrasted and combined cognitive-behavioral and medication treatments for problems in social interactions, including anger and aggression (Hinshaw, Henker, & Whalen, 1984a, 1984b).

Most of my work for over 20 years has, in fact, focused on children with such difficulties. I have long been interested in the developmental processes that led to these conditions, including biological and neuropsychological risk factors, as well as family and peer influences. I do much of my research in summer camps that I direct; these allow me and my research team to observe children's behavior in natural, as opposed to artificial, settings and to study the development of peer relations and friendships without the constraint of their prior reputations. More recently, I have begun to examine brain functions of such children in functional MRI studies, to follow the youngsters into adolescence and adulthood through prospective longitudinal research, and to join up with other investigators in large-scale treatment trials (such as the Multimodal Treatment Study of Children with ADHD; e.g., MTA Cooperative Group, 1999; Hinshaw et al., 2000). What is truly exciting is to be able to blend developmental psychology, clinical psychology, social-personality psychology, cognitive theories of attention and other processes of the mind, and neuroscience methods in the multidisciplinary studies I perform.

Over and above the content of this research, however, what now stands out to me are the reasons that I began to work with children and families and to pursue a career in clinical psychology. While in college, during winter holidays and spring breaks I would return home to Ohio. Surprisingly at first, my father began to pull me aside for a series of talks about his life. This was a new experience for me, because I simply didn't know much of his history before that time. I knew him as a warm but intellectual dad who was a professor of philosophy at Ohio State. On occasion, when my sister and I were young, my father would disappear for several months or longer; but my parents never spoke a word of these instances. His behavior was sometimes erratic, and at other times he seemed preoccupied and "out of it," but I had learned not to ask. Indeed, I spent a lot of my childhood and adolescence immersed in sports and schoolwork, trying to avoid thinking about it.

But when my father began his talks with me, he told me of his experiences as an adolescent, when he was put into the back wards of a mental hospital for six months, following his attempt to "fly" from the roof of this family home in California, emanating from an irrational desire to tell the world to stop Hitler and Mussolini. And he told me of later hospitalizations, too, all of which emanated from intense, psychotic episodes. Several of the worst of these occurred when my sister and I were young. In fact, when I was in third grade, my father was gone for an entire year, hospitalized in California, with his brother (a psychiatrist) helping to coordinate his care. He had carried, since his initial hospitalization at age sixteen, a diagnosis of schizophrenia, and he had received antipsychotic medications plus a series of electroconvulsive therapy treatments (ECTs) for many years. I also learned that my father's doctors had cautioned him never to tell my sister or me about his episodes or experiences because "children cannot understand mental illness." My mother, who stood by my father for his entire adult life, had no choice but to go along. At the same time, without her strength, the family could never have stayed together.

After my father finally rejected this advice when I began college, his talks opened up a whole new world to me, one of fascination with his intense psychological experiences, but also one of real anxiety as I wondered whether I myself was doomed to become psychotic and go to a mental hospital. Little wonder that I gravitated to working with children and to the field of psychology: I wanted to learn about the mind and about how to help children and families cope with mental illness.

After college, I read more scientific literature and realized that my father actually suffered from manic-depressive illness (bipolar disorder). I helped him to get rediagnosed and, forty years after his initial episode, treated with lithium. Although he had some years of relief, he had already begun a gradual decline in his cognitive functioning, and his latter years were not marked by the same brilliance he had shown early on. Still, his warmth and sensitivity persisted.

As part of the requirements for a clinical psychology Ph.D., one performs a year-long clinical internship. Mine was at the Neuropsychiatric Institute of UCLA, where I was supervised by Kay Redfield Jamison at the Affective

Disorders Clinic. This was years before her own disclosure about her life-long bipolar disorder (Jamison, 1995), but the seminar she conducted let me know that thousands of individuals in the United States had been mis-diagnosed with schizophrenia from the 1930s through the 1960s. I thus realized that my father's story was important historically and clinically.

After years of struggling with my own silence and shame about my father's condition, I finally decided to write a book about his life and my relationship with him. As I began the initial drafts, I discussed the project with my father, who, despite his late-life Parkinson's disease, gave me his permission to write it, a few months before he passed away. In *The Years of Silence: My Father's Life with Bipolar Disorder* (Hinshaw, 2002), I chronicle his many struggles and personal triumphs, at the same time discussing several core issues about mental health: the need for accurate diagnosis and responsive treatment, the complex genetic and psychological triggers for serious conditions like bi-polar disorder, and as the strength and resilience (beyond the shame and despair) that mental illness can yield.

Since my coming to terms with my father's life and my family legacy, which includes strong genetic tendencies for mental illness interspersed with high achievement, nearly everything in my life has become richer. My teaching is infused with a new openness about mental illness, which enhances discussion of the field's scientific efforts to overcome mental disorder. My research has expanded to include, over and above my continuing work in developmental psychopathology, interest in why mental illness continues to be so strongly stigmatized in our supposedly enlightened era. New books on the stigma of mental illness (including means of enhancing family communication), and on personal and family experience of mental disorders, are forthcoming.

I feel incredibly fortunate to be living in an era in which the current ex-plosion of scientific knowledge about all aspects of psychology, and mental illness in particular, is increasingly combined with openness, communication, and compassion. The hope is that the most rigorous research studies will blend with deep human concern in order to help end the silence and shame that still surround mental illness. With the recent gains in knowledge about both genes and life experiences, it is essential that the best young minds in our society understand the importance of psychology and mental health. Psychology offers all of us the potential to expand our compassion for all members of society, particularly persons and family members who experience the ravages of mental illness. The journey will be long but well worth the efforts involved.

The concluding story in this book relates psychology to passion. This section by bestselling text book writer David Myers, Ph.D., Professor,

Hope College, details the convictions, and lessons learned throughout his career.

Passionate Teaching and Lessons Learned
David G. Myers

Having recently completed three-and-a-half decades professing psychology and having passed sixty years of age, I see this as a fitting time to reflect again on some lessons I have learned. Perhaps this self-disclosure can stimulate some of you to reflect on the lessons you have learned while professing psychology, and hopefully those students who are just beginning their career journey. These "lessons" can perhaps be best articulated by what Bob Sternberg (i.e., Robert Sternberg, Ph.D., professor, Yale University) calls your "tacit knowledge"—the implicit, experienced-based principles that facilitate your work life.

CAREER AND LIFE LESSONS

Lesson 1: One Cannot Predict the Future

As an undergraduate chemistry major who had taken only introductory psychology during my first three years, I never would have guessed that I would become a social psychologist. When entering graduate school, aiming to become a college teacher, I never would have guessed that I would become engaged by research. When doing research during my assistant professor years, I never would have guessed that I would become a writer.

The awakening of my interest in social psychological research illustrates why I have come to expect the unexpected. When I arrived to begin Iowa's graduate program in 1964, having declared my interest in personality, my advisor explained that the department's one faculty member in personality had just left. "So we've put you in social psychology"—that is how I became a social psychologist.

During my second year, I assisted social psychologist Sidney Aronson by engaging forty small groups in discussing story problems that assessed risk taking. We replicated the phenomenon of increased risk taking by groups, dubbed the "risky shift," and before long this college teacher wanna-be had, to his surprise, also become a research psychologist. Moreover, the research mutated unpredictably—from risky shift to a broader group polarization phenomenon to studies of the subtle influence on attitudes of mere exposure to others' attitudes.

Lesson 2: Contrarian Professional Investment Can Pay Big Dividends

Major contributions often occur when people invest in a research problem at an early stage—when, as Bob Sternberg says, "the intellectual stock is still undervalued." Unless you are uncommonly brilliant, which most of us are not, a good way to contribute to psychology is to pick a research problem that has received little study. This strategy offers the chance to master the available literature before it proceeds to third-order interaction effects. Then stay with the stock—become a world-class expert. The risky-shift, group polarization literature was visited by dozens of people who dabbled with a study or two and then moved on to do a study or two in other areas. The people who really enlarged our understanding were not these researchers, but those who stayed around long enough to dive deep, often by offering a single idea that they pushed to its limits.

Lesson 3: Scholarship Can Be a Lonely Enterprise

When you have freshly mastered a literature topic and know it about as well as anyone in the world, few other people may know or care. Unless one is working on a team project, to be a scholar is often to feel alone and ignored. Once we have done our research, written it up, endured the publication lag, had our work cited in secondary sources, and gone on to other things, *then* people will take us to be experts and may invite us to give talks and write reflective chapters. Meanwhile, the fresh minds working at the cutting edge will be languishing for such opportunities.

Lesson 4: Success, Even If Serendipitous, Builds on Itself

Life is not fair. Success biases new opportunities toward those who have already been given other opportunities. Although the skills required for research and for writing overlap only modestly, it was my good fortune to happen onto what turned out to be a fruitful research problem that led to an invitation to write my social psychology text, which led to an invitation to write an introductory psychology text, which lent credibility to my approach to a literary agent about writing *The Pursuit of Happiness* (1993), which opened doors for other opportunities to communicate psychological science to the lay public. Although the process begins with solitary hard work, fortunate outcomes can lead to more opportunities, whether you are the most deserving person or not. Success feeds on itself. So it pays to start well.

Lesson 5: To Be an Effective, Contributing Professional One Need Not Be Uncommonly Brilliant or Creative

With dogged work, I was able to master a literature topic and connect some dots, despite not having the genius to invent the theories. You need not be as theoretically creative as Nobel Laureate cognitive psychologist Daniel Kahneman to work at winnowing truth from falsehood, at consolidating what we have learned, or at communicating it to college students and the lay public. That is what Dean Simonton (1994) has discerned from the curvilinear relationship between intelligence and leadership ability. Up to a point, intelligence facilitates leadership. However, an excessive intellectual gap between leader and follower can hamper their communication. Good teaching and science writing likewise require enough intelligence to comprehend what the pioneering theorists are saying and discovering, but not so much that one is out of touch with how ordinary people think and talk.

If you are not brilliant or expert on every aspect of a problem, it also helps to gain the support of people whose competencies complement your own. I suspect every text author has at times felt mildly embarrassed by people who are too impressed—people who think we just sat down and wrote what they are reading, assuming they never could. Such folks should not be so intimidated. It actually took a whole team of reviewers and editors to shape, over several drafts, a work that surpasses what the author, working alone, was capable of writing.

Lesson 6: You Do Not Get Pellets Unless You Press the Bar

Life has us on partial reinforcement schedules. What one reviewer thinks is pointless research, another will think is pioneering. What one reader finds "too cute," another will find refreshingly witty. The poet Pennington was once rejected by a magazine that explained, "This is the worst poem in the English language. You are the worst poet in the English language." So he sent the poem to another magazine, which accepted it "with glowing praise" and chose it as its year's best poem.

Given the unreliability of others' judgments of our work, it pays to try and try again. Our colleagues who are athletic coaches live with the publicity given both their victories and their defeats. Those of us who are scholars only announce our victories. However, let me admit to one of my strings of unpublicized defeats. Several years ago, *Today's Education* rejected my critique of the labeling and segregation of "gifted" children from the 95 percent of children deemed, by implication, "ungifted." I then submitted it to six other periodicals, all of which rejected it. Noticing that *Today's Education* by now had a new editor, and thinking the piece slightly improved, I resubmitted it to *Today's Education* without reminding them that they had already rejected a previous draft. They accepted it immediately, published it, later gave permission for its reprinting in newspapers and magazines, and invited me to write more!

Lesson 7: If You Feel Excited by an Idea or a Possibility, Do Not Be Deterred by Criticism

We have all heard stories of great books that were rejected countless times before publication, or works of art or music that went unappreciated during the creator's lifetime. People derided Robert Fulton's steamboat as "Fulton's Folly." As Fulton later said, "Never did a single encouraging remark, a bright hope, a warm wish, cross my path." Much the same reaction greeted the printing press, the telegraph, the incandescent lamp, and the typewriter. John White's book *Rejection* (1982) is one story after another of all the scorn and derision that greeted the work of people from Michelangelo and Beethoven to the American poet A. Wilber Stevens, who received from his hoped-for publisher an envelope of ashes. Remember, Dr. Seuss was initially rejected by some two dozen publishers! "There is no way to sell a book about an unknown Dutch painter," Doubleday explained before Irving Stone's book about Van Gogh (1963) survived fifteen rejections and reportedly sold 25 million copies. In a possibly apocryphal story, one of the seven publishers that rejected *The Tale of Peter Rabbit* said that the tale "smelled like rotting carrots."

If you pick up brochures for anyone's textbook and read all the nice quotations, you may feel a twinge of envy, thinking it must be nice to get all those glowing reviews—those are not all the reviews. Let me tell you about some reviews that you will never see quoted. One long-retired reviewer of my introductory psychology text offered the following in his chapter reviews:

> The use of the English language in this book is atrocious. Faulty grammar and syntax, imprecise meaning and incorrect terminology etc. etc. are abundant. When I'm reading the book I have the feeling that it is written by one of my undergraduate students; when reviewing this edition it is at times like correcting an undergraduate term paper.

In response to another chapter he wrote that

> I find the tone and even content paternalistic, value laden and maybe even demeaning. Especially the section on "work" is very poor; it left

me angry that one would want to present such "crap" to learning young adults. Did Dr. Myers really write this vague, stereotypical, poorly worded, unclear and confusing section on work?

Yet another chapter: "At times this text reads as if it has been a translation from the German language." (Incredibly, this reviewer, who also had helpful suggestions, shortly thereafter adopted the book.)

Then there was the reviewer who noted that the book "is very biased and opinionated. I don't think the author is very competent. I have thought of writing a text and perhaps now more so," whereupon he proceeded to offer his services.

While preparing that book's first edition, there were days when, after being hammered on by editors—one of whom scribbled criticism all over several chapters with but *one* still-remembered compliment: "nice simile"—I longed for a single encouraging word. One of my most difficult professional tasks—perhaps yours, too, as you cope with mentors' criticisms, professional reviews, or student evaluations—is being open to feedback without feeling defeated by it. The lesson I have learned from this is this: Listen to criticism, but if you have a vision, hold to it. Keep your eye on the goal. In retrospect, I am glad I submitted to the process, but I am also glad I did not let it intimidate me into submission.

Lesson 8: As Praise and Criticism Accumulate, Their Power to Elate or Depress Lessen

Compliments provoke less elation, and criticisms less despair, as both become mere iotas of additional feedback atop a pile of accumulated praise and reproach. That helps explain why emotions mellow as we age. I have spent hours in sleepless anguish over my children's ups and downs, but rarely, of late, over professional criticism. As Albert Ellis (i.e, Albert Ellis, Ph.D., pioneer of rational-emotive therapy) keeps reminding people, not everyone is going to love what we do. The more feedback I receive, the more I can accept that.

Lesson 9: Achievement Comes with Keeping Focused and Managing Time

Our basketball coaches say their teams play well when they keep their focus, without being distracted from their game plan by the referees' calls, the opposing fans, or the other team's spurts. A successful entrepreneur friend speaks of achieving success by keeping his focus—knowing his niche, where he is needed, what he is good at. We all get asked to do all sorts of things that other people can do as well or better. My experience is that the world is a better place when each of us identifies and then focuses on our best gifts. When a service club wants a talk on a topic where I have no expertise, or when a caller needs a counselor, I decline, with thanks, or offer a referral, remembering that every time I say yes to something I am implicitly saying no to some other use of that time. Sometimes I want to say yes to that use of time, which is what led me to spend time preparing these reflections. Other times, the alternative uses of the time feel like higher priorities.

When my house needed repair work, I tried, even when supporting a family solely on an assistant professor's income, to emulate my father, who would pay craftspeople to do what they could do better and more efficiently, which gave them work and freed his time for his profession. In the long run, it has paid off. I am not advocating a workaholism that competes with investing in family relationships, relaxing hobbies, and an equitable sharing of daily domestic work; if I can focus all those other hours on the professional work that I most enjoy, I will have more to give. It is a point I make to younger colleagues when I see them doing clerical work, which both deprives someone else of a job and steals time from their own profession.

Time management also pays dividends. Several years ago I noticed one of my colleagues writing down something in his desk calendar as someone left his office. What was he doing? He was logging his time, he explained, to see how closely his use of time mirrored his espoused priorities. I decided to do the same.

What a revelation! Not only did I learn how long it took me to write a textbook—3,550 hours for the first edition of *Social Psychology*—but also I learned how poorly my actual priorities matched my proclaimed priorities. More minutes adding up to more hours than I would have believed were frittered away uselessly—not counseling students, not teaching, not doing research or writing, not in meetings, just doing nothing useful. While still allowing time for spontaneous connections with people, that very realization made me more conscious of wasted time.

Another time management strategy is to set big goals, then break them down into weekly objectives. Before beginning work on a new textbook, I would lay out a week-by-week schedule. My goal was not to have the whole 600-page book done by such and such date; that is too remote and formidable, but writing three manuscript pages a day is a relative cuppa tea. Repeat the process 400 times and, presto! you have a 1,200-page manuscript. It is really not so hard, nor is reaching many goals when attacked day by day. Although we often overestimate how much we will accomplish in any given day, we generally underestimate how much we can accomplish in a year, given just a little progress every day. Moreover, as each mini-deadline is met, one gets the delicious, confident feeling of personal control.

Lesson 10: Success Requires Enough Optimism to Provide Hope and Enough Pessimism to Prevent Complacency

Feeling capable of but one task at a time partly reflects a nagging lack of self-confidence, the sort of "defensive pessimism" that, ironically, can enable success—when it goads us to believe that only by utter diligence will we ever do work on a par with that done by all those more brilliant people at more famous places. It was because I knew I was not a gifted writer (my worst college grade was in a writing class) that I focused on developing my writing skills—by reading great writers such as C. S. Lewis and Carl Sagan; by studying style manuals such as Strunk and White's *Elements of Style* (2000), Jacques Barzun's *Simple and Direct* (2001), and William Zinsser's *On Writing Well* (2001); by subjecting my writing to a computer grammar checker; and, especially, by engaging a writing coach—a poet colleague who has closely edited some 5,000 of my manuscript pages while patiently teaching me what it means to develop a voice, to order words to maximize punch, to write with rhythm. It pays to have enough self-confidence to risk undertaking a project, and enough self-doubt to think you will fail if you do not focus enormous effort on it.

IMPLICATIONS FOR TEACHERS AND TEACHING

Each of these lessons, born of experience, have implications for teachers and teaching.

Teaching Implication for Lesson 1

The future's unpredictability provides a rationale for liberal education. You cannot know your future, I explain to new and prospective students—"Your interests on entering college will likely change during college, and change again during your working life." Most students end up majoring in something they did not have in mind on entering college, and end up in a vocation unrelated to their major. That is why a broad education for an unpredictable future—a liberal education—serves most students better than a purely vocational education.

Teaching Implication for Lesson 2

Contrarian investment sometimes pays dividends, not only when placed in undervalued financial and intellectual stocks, but also in undervalued or undeveloped students. We teachers take joy in spotting and encouraging potential talent in students whose minds are just now awakening to the world of learning. I came to college with an above average but undistinguished high school record and interests that barely ranged beyond sports, salmon fishing, and the family business. But thanks in part to Whitworth College faculty that opened my mind to interesting ideas and encouraged me to believe in my own potential, my interests expanded and, much to my surprise, four years later I found myself in graduate school.

Teaching Implication for Lesson 3

Teaching, like scholarship, can be a lonely enterprise. "When preparing classes and facing students we're usually on our own." My college has responded to this reality with a week-long August "teaching enhancement" workshop for new faculty. Not only are they exposed to some effective teaching strategies, they gain a senior faculty mentor (who plays no part in assessing them for tenure), and they immediately gain a support group of friends who are part of their pledge class of newcomers.

Teaching Implication for Lesson 4

Teaching success, like scholarly success, feeds on itself. With success comes increased comfort and confidence, which breeds further success, which builds one's reputation, which heightens students' expectations as they enter your class. Students often begin courses having heard "Professor Smith is interesting" and "Professor Jones is a bore." Robert Feldman (Feldman & Prohaska, 1979; Feldman & Theiss, 1982) found that such expectations can affect both student and teacher. Students in a learning experiment who expected to be taught by a competent teacher perceived their teacher (who was unaware of their expectations) as more competent and interesting than did students with low expectations. Furthermore, the students actually learned more. In a follow-up experiment, Feldman and Prohaska videotaped teachers and had observers later rate their performance. Teachers were judged most capable when assigned a student who nonverbally conveyed positive expectations.

To see whether such effects might also occur in actual classrooms, a research team led by David Jamieson (1987) experimented with four Ontario high school classes taught by a newly transferred teacher. During individual interviews they told students in two of the classes that both other students and the research team rated the teacher very highly. Compared to the control classes, the students given positive expectations paid better attention during class. At the end of the teaching unit, they also got better grades and rated the teacher as clearer in her teaching. The attitudes that a class has toward its teacher are as important, it seems, as the teacher's attitude toward the students.

Teaching Implication for Lesson 5

Effectiveness does not require uncommon brilliance or creativity. Some of our colleagues have the genius to invent great ideas and do pioneering research. If others of us lack the smarts or resources to match their intellectual accomplishments, we may nonetheless be smart enough to take the bread that's baking up in the ivory towers and bring it down to the street where folks can eat it. Moreover, some of us may have gifts of warmth, enthusiasm, and passion for teaching that enable us to communicate psychology more effectively than can our most distinguished psychological scientists. Many leading scientists understand this and therefore appreciate those who effectively give their work away to the public.

Teaching Implication for Lesson 6

Teachers, too, get partial reinforcement for bar pressing. Some demonstrations, some jokes, some media, some lectures, some discussion topics flop. Others *really* work! The point is effectively made. Students are engaged and participating. As we try new activities and get reinforced for the things that do work, our courses gradually mutate to greater and greater effectiveness (assuming we maintain our freshness and enthusiasm).

Teaching Implication for Lesson 7

Great teachers are informed but not deflated by criticism. Feedback—the more specific, the better—is part of the process by which students reinforce and strengthen what we do well, and inform us of what needs redoing. Even very good teachers get wounded by stinging criticism from a few anonymous students. And so do all of us. Here, from my files, is an example from one student's end-of-course evaluation:

What did you find beneficial about this course:
  "Nothing."

If you think that the course could be improved, what would you suggest:
  "End the course."

What advice would you give to a friend who is planning to take this course?
  "Don't."

Because we hold such comments to ourselves, we may be unaware that our esteemed colleagues occasionally get similarly stung.

Teaching Implication for Lesson 8

As student feedback accumulates, its power to elate or depress wanes. If the nasty feedback above had been in response to my first teaching effort, I might have contemplated my father's invitation to come home to Seattle to join the family insurance agency. Coming after many semesters of teaching, after receiving feedback from many hundreds of students, a single statement of praise ("this is the best class and best teacher I have ever had") still feels good, and a single hostile statement ("the course was dull and the tests unfair") still feels bad. But one's head doesn't swell over the former (we know not all students responded so warmly), nor does the sting of a single criticism cause a sleepless night.

Teaching Implication for Lesson 9

Teaching success comes with focus and time management. It comes with identifying and harnessing our gifts (are we especially good at lecturing? facilitating discussion? engaging students with activities and media?). And it comes with teaching multiple sections of a few courses (as opposed to single sections of many courses). Noting that it took emotional energy to gear up for class and to descend after class, I bunched my classes together into Tuesdays and Thursdays—leaving the other days emotionally freer to concentrate on research and writing. Having multiple sections of the same course—teaching, if possible, all my social psychology sections one semester, all my introductory psychology sections another—further reduced the work load without compromising the teaching load. By clustering our year's sections of a given course in one semester, we reduce the number of preparations (and of sets of lectures, exams, media hassles, and trips to the Xerox machine) in any one semester.

Teaching Implication for Lesson 10

Teaching success grows from a mix of confidence-enabling optimism and defensive pessimism. To feel comfortable and in command of our material and presentation, we've got to believe in our competence and teaching skill. Yet a dash of anxiety both motivates preparation and lends a certain edge. Just before meeting my first class of the day I would always find my autonomic nervous system requiring a last-minute visit to the bathroom (a phenomenon that other colleagues experience as well). That pre-class arousal is part of the edge, the energy, the enthusiasm that enables our best teaching.

Bibliography

Barzun, J. (2001). *Simple and direct (4th Ed.)*. New York: HarperPerennial.

Berkowitz, L., & Lepage, A. (1967). Weapons as aggression-eliciting stimuli. *Journal of Personality and Social Psychology*, 7, 202–207.

Chamberlain, J. (2004, January). Words from the wise: Seasoned and early-career professionals share their tips for a fruitful psychology career. *gradPSYCH*, 2, 1.

Dittman, M. (2003, September). CV dos and don'ts. *gradPSYCH*, 1, 2.

Feldman, R. S., & Prohaska, T. R. (1979). The student as Pygmalion: Effects of student expectation on the teacher. *Journal of Educational Psychology*, 71, 485–493.

Feldman, R. S., & Theiss, A. J. (1982). The teacher and student as pygmalions: Joint effects of teacher and student expectations. *Journal of Educational Psychology*, 74, 217–223.

Flavell, J. H. (1962). *The developmental psychology of Jean Piaget*. New York: van Nostrand Reinhold.

Gilligan, C. (1993). *In a different voice: Psychological theory and women's development*. Boston: Harvard University Press.

Hinshaw, S. P. (2002). *The years of silence are past: My father's life with bipolar disorder*. New York: Cambridge University Press.

Hinshaw, S. P., Henker, B., & Whalen, C. K. (1984a). Self control in hyperactive boys in anger inducing situations: Effects of cognitive-behavioral training and of methylphenidate. *Journal of Abnormal Child Psychology*, 12, 55–77.

Hinshaw, S. P., Henker, B., & Whalen, C. K. (1984b). Cognitive behavioral and pharmacologic interventions for hyperactive boys: Comparative and combined effects. *Journal of Consulting and Clinical Psychology*, 52, 739–749.

Hinshaw, S. P., Owens, E. B., Wells, K. C., Kraemer, H. C., Abikoff, H. B., Arnold, L. E., Conners, C. K., Elliott, G., Greenhill, L. L., Hechtman, L., Hoza, B., Jensen, P. S., March, J. S., Newcorn, J., Pelham, W. E., Swanson, J. M., Vitiello, B., & Wigal, T. (2000). Family processes and treatment outcome in the MTA: Negative/ineffective parenting practices in relation to multimodal treatment. *Journal of Abnormal Child Psychology*, *28*, 555–568.

Jamieson, D. W., Lydon, J. E., Stewart, G., & Zanna, M. P. (1987). Pygmalion revisited: New evidence for student expectancy effects in the classroom. *Journal of Educational Psychology*, *79*, 461–466.

Jamison, K. R. (1995). *An unquiet mind: A memoir of moods and madness*. New York: Knopf.

Lahey, B. (2003). *Psychology: An introduction (8th Ed.)*. New York: McGraw-Hill.

Morgan, B. L., & Korschgen, A. (2001, Spring). Psychology career exploration made easy: Using the Web to do the job. *Eye on Psi Chi*, *5*, 35–36.

Morris, C. G., & Maisto, A. A. (2004). *Psychology: An introduction (12th Ed.)*. New York: Prentice Hall.

MTA Cooperative Group. (1999). Fourteen-month randomized clinical trial of treatment strategies for attention-deficit hyperactivity disorder. *Archives of General Psychiatry*, *56*, 1073–1086.

Murray, B. (1998, January). PhDs apply talents to emerging careers. *APA Monitor*, *29*(1).

Myers, D. G. (2003). *Psychology (7th Ed.)*. New York: Worth.

Myers, D. G. (1993). *The pursuit of happiness*. New York: Harper.

Nietzel, M. T., Bernstein, D. A., Kramer, G. P., & Milich, R. (2003). *Introduction to clinical psychology (6th Ed.)*. New York: Prentice Hall.

Oster, G., & Montgomery, S. (1994). *Helping your depressed teenager: A guide for parents and caregivers*. New York: Wiley.

Overmier, J. B., & Seligman, M.E.P. (1967). Effects of inescapable shock upon subsequent escape and avoidance responding. *Journal of Comparative Physiological Psychology*, *63*, 28–33.

Peterson, C., Maier, S. F., & Seligman, M.E.P. (1995). *Learned helplessness: A theory for the age of personal control*. New York: Oxford University Press.

Simonton, D. K. (1994). *Greatness: Who makes history and why*. New York: Guilford.

Smith, M. B. (2003). *For a significant social psychology: The collected writings of M. Brewster Smith*. New York: New York University Press.

Stone, I. (1963). *Lust for life: The story of Vincent Van Gogh*. New York: Pocket Books.

Strunk, W., White, E. B., & Angell, R. (2000). *The elements of style (4th Ed.)*.
    New York: Longman.
White, J. (1982). *Rejection*. New York: Addison-Wesley.
Zinsser, W. (2001). *On writing well*. New York: Collins.

Suggested Readings

American Psychological Association (1993). *Getting In: A step-by-step plan for gaining admission to graduate school in psychology.* Washington, D.C.: APA Books. This exceptional guide leads the undergraduate major through a careful self-assessment to determine the skills and interests that will guide the applicant's choice of graduate education. Chapters that detail career options, licensure issues, and the application process are thorough reminders that planning is important. Checklists and timelines are provided for assistance.

American Psychological Association (2005). *Graduate study in psychology 2006.* Washington, D.C.: APA Books. An updated version, this comprehensive guide offers complete practical information about over 500 psychology programs in the United States and Canada. This edition provides current facts about programs and degrees offered, admission requirements, financial aid, and housing.

DeGalan, Julie, & Lambert, Stephen (2000). *Great jobs for psychology majors.* New York: McGraw-Hill. This book includes basic information, for instance, how to write a resume and cover letter and interviewing procedures. The authors also include an overview of the history of psychology and its evolution into newer areas of family, forensics, and women studies.

Kuther, Tara L., & Morgan, Robert D. (2003). *Careers in Psychology: Opportunities in a changing world.* New York: Wadsworth Publishing. *Careers in Psychology* helps students answer the pragmatic questions that many psychology majors ask while still in college. The authors encourage students to take an active role in their own career planning, to take control of their education, and to further define their career goals within psychology.

Landrum, R. Eric, & Davis, Stephen F. (2003). *The psychology major: Career options and strategies for success* (2nd Ed.). New York: Prentice Hall. The authors of this book provide strategies for success that will allow students better opportunities to achieve their career goals. Their purpose is to provide useful and helpful information to students majoring in psychology, such as how to do well in classes, how to find research ideas, and the need to look at future salaries within psychology-related careers. Other benefits include sections on self-reflection, writing papers in APA style, and examining ethics within the psychology profession.

Morgan, Betsy L., & Korschgen, Ann (2005). *Majoring in psych? Career options for psychology majors* (3rd Ed.). New York: Allyn & Bacon. This book focuses on the multiple ways students can enhance their marketability while still in school. In order to demystify the process of career development, this guide answers the career-planning questions most psychology majors find themselves asking.

O'Hara, Shelley (2005). *What can you do with a major in psychology? Real people. Real jobs. Real rewards.* New York: Cliff Notes. This guide offers information on college choices and internships, as well as tips to help you land a job. There are profiles of real graduates and descriptions of their jobs and how they got them. An array of career options are explored, including art therapy and criminal investigation. Additional resources include websites, professional organizations, and licensing requirements.

Prinstein, Mitchell J., & Patterson, Marcus (Eds.) (2003). *The portable mentor: Expert guide to a successful career in psychology*. New York: Plenum. This book was designed to combine the knowledge of a wide range of noted psychologists whose training and experience provide the reader with an abundance of insight. Based on real-life concerns of students and beginning professionals, this text takes readers from psychology graduate school to their journey into career development. The volume covers tips on teaching, grant writing, publishing research, and starting clinical practices.

Sayette, Michael A., Mayne, Tracy J., & Norcross, John C. (2004). *Insider's guide to graduate programs in clinical and counseling psychology*. New York: Guilford Press. An excellent resource for anyone considering applying to graduate programs in clinical or counseling psychology, this book is a step-by-step guide on how to gain admission to your desired school.

It includes advice on which classes to take, direction for research experiences, and practical matters such as costs. It also provides detailed information on nearly 300 graduate programs.

Sternberg, Robert J. (Ed.) (1997). *Career paths in psychology*. Washington, D.C.: APA Books. In this volume, Robert Sternberg lends his name to a collection of articles covering the fourteen major career options in psychology. Each contributor has been hugely successful in his or her niche and, accordingly, elevates opportunities. The fourteen careers include academia (separate chapters on the different academic departments such as psychology, school psychology, and business), counseling (private practices, schools, community organizations, and hospitals are covered in separate chapters), government research, public school work, industrial and organizational psychology, consumer psychology, human-factors psychology, military psychology, and health psychology.

Super, Donald E., & Super, C. (2001). *Opportunities in psychology careers*. New York: McGraw-Hill. *Opportunities in Psychology Careers* offers job seekers essential information about a variety of careers in the field of psychology. This concise book allows the reader to see what it will take to succeed in a career in psychology. The book includes training and education requirements, salary statistics, and professional and internet resources. Sufficent analysis of these subjects as well as specialities in the field of psychology all provide a good general summary of what a career in this area of study will entail.

Relevant Websites

Academy for Behavioral Profiling (www.profiling.org). Provides in-depth education in evidence-based crime analysis, describing actual practices and discussing public awareness about the topic.

Academy for the Study of Psychoanalytic Arts (www.academyanalyticarts .org). Aims to further the research of psychoanalytic epistemology and practice through the eyes of philosophy as opposed to biology.

American Academy of Child and Adolescent Psychiatry (www.aacap.org). Helps families understand and cope with the developmental difficulties of their children. The website offers stories and facts that can be useful to such families.

American Academy of Counseling Psychology (www.aacop.net). Promotes counseling psychology as a legitimate practice of psychology.

American Art Therapy Association (www.arttherapy.org). National association that thrives on creativity as a helpful tool toward recovery and therapy.

American Association for Correctional Psychology (www.eaacp.org). Organization of behavioral scientists and practitioners who are concerned with the delivery of high-quality mental health services to criminal offenders.

American Music Therapy Association (www.musictherapy.org). Official website that provides information about professional requirements and careers in music therapy, in addition to identifying practice concerns.

American Psychiatric Association (www.psych.org). Worldwide medical society that works toward better treatment for those with mental disabilities, including substance abuse and retardation.

American Psychiatric Nurses Association (www.apna.org). Promotes the field of psychiatric nursing and works to develop the health care policies within psychiatry.

American Psychological Association (www.apa.org). Official site describing the profession of psychology and offering tips about getting into graduate school. This site also shares APA book titles as well as its monthly newsletter.

American Psychological Association of Graduate Students (www.apa.org/apags). Has active membership of more than 30,000 graduate and undergraduate students in psychology.

American Psychological Society (www.psychologicalscience.org). National nonprofit organization dedicated to enhancing scientific research for psychology.

Applied Experimental and Engineering (www.apa.org/divisions/div21). Provides counseling services and networking opportunities to those interested in pursuing careers in applied experimental or engineering psychology.

Asian Association of Social Psychology (www.asiansocialpsych.org). Has roughly 400 members and publishes the *Asian Journal of Social Psychology*.

Association for the Advancement of Applied Sport Psychology (www.aaas ponline.org). Offers extensive information for the public about applied psychology, sports psychology, health and exercise psychology, and the like.

Association of Black Psychologists (www.abpsi.org). Has more than 1,400 members who promote social change and assist African American communities and other ethnic groups.

Disability Mentoring Program (www.apa.org/pi/cdip/mentoring/homepage .html). Supports psychology students with disabilities in their academic and professional career by linking them with a mentor who also has a disability.

Graduate Record Exam (www.gre.org). Contains all the information you will need in planning to take the GRE, including practice tests, receiving feedback, and obtaining information about accommodations.

International Association of Cross-Cultural Psychology (www.iaccp.org). Has more than 500 members in sixty-five countries.

International Society of Political Psychology (ispp.org). Represents all fields of inquiry concerned with exploring the relationship between political and psychological processes. Members are from across disciplines.

Internet Mental Health (www.mentalhealth.com). Provides education on a variety of mental illnesses, their possible treatments, different hopeful stories, and much more.

Lesbian, Gay, Bisexual, and Transgender Mentoring Program (www.apa .org/apags/diversity/stucover.html). Matches lesbian, gay, bisexual, and transgender (LGBT) graduate students in psychology with a doctoral-level mentor to provide guidance, support, and networking through a joint mentoring program run by the APAGS Committee on Lesbian, Gay, Bisexual, and Transgender Concerns.

NAMI: National Alliance for the Mentally Ill (www.nami.org). Educates the world about mental illness to relieve the pre-existing stigma of those with mental illnesses and to help with the integration of the mentally ill into society.

National Association of School Psychologists (NASP) (nasponline.org). Promotes the education and betterment of those with mental illnesses.

National Coalition of Art Therapies Association (www.ncata.com). Boast a coalition of six various art therapies: art therapy, dance and movement therapy, drama therapy, music therapy, poetry therapy, and psycho-drama.

National Institute of Mental Health (www.nimh.nih.gov). Federal agency that researches mental and behavioral disorders.

National Institutes of Health (www.nih.gov). Official website for one of the foremost research centers.

National Membership Committee on Psychoanalysis in Clinical Social Work (www.nmcop.org). Promulgates using psychoanalysis in social work.

National Mental Health Association (www.nmha.org). Oldest nonprofit organization in the United States dealing with the severe issues of mental illnesses.

North American Society for the Psychology of Sport and Physical Activity (www.naspspa.org). Works to enhance the research of human behavior in sports and physical activity.

Occupational Health Psychology, National Institute for Occupational Safety and Health (www.cdc.gov/niosh/ohp.html). Researches stress found in the occupational realm and works on prevention of injury, stress, and the like, in occupations.

Peace, War, and Social Conflict, a section of the American Sociological Association (www.peacewarconflict.org). Official site for association dealing with issues of peace, war, and social conflict. Offers featured speakers and various conventions.

Psi Chi (www.psichi.org). National Honor Society in Psychology.

Psychonomic Society (www.psychonomic.org). Promotes the communication of scientific research in psychology and allied sciences. The society publishes journals on topics of learning, memory, and psychophysics.

Society for Industrial and Organizational Psychology (www.siop.org). Hopes to enhance human well-being and performance in work settings by promoting the science, practice, and teaching of industrial and organizational psychology.

Society for Personality and Social Psychology (www.spsp.org). Has more than 4,000 members and publishes prominent journals in the field.

Society for the Psychological Study of Social Issues (www.spssi.org). Has more than 3,000 members and focuses on societal problems.

Society for the Psychology of Women (www.apa.org/divisions/div35). Provides a student editorial board for *Psychology of Women Quarterly*, in which advanced graduate students can serve under a consulting editor or associate editor to learn about the review and editorial process.

Society for the Study of Peace, Conflict, and Violence: Peace Psychology (www.webster.edu/peacepsychology). An organization comprised of faculty, students, and the public to offer their insight and perspectives on peace.

Society for the Teaching of Psychology Mentoring Service (www.psynt.iupui .edu/MentoringService). Offers a mentoring service for teachers of psychology to ask questions to more experienced colleagues about classroom management and topics as well as career guidance.

Women in Science and Technology e-Mentor Program (www.apa.org/ science/wist/mentor.html). Offers an e-mentoring program through APA's Science Directorate that provides guidance for women pursuing careers in science and technology.

Index

About the Author
and Contributors

GERALD D. OSTER, Ph.D., is currently in full-time private practice in Olney and Rockville, Maryland, providing therapeutic interventions to a wide range of children, adults, and families. He is a former Clinical Associate Professor of Psychiatry at the University of Maryland Medical School, as well as past Director of Psychology Internship Training. He has co-authored books on psychological testing (*Assessing Adolescents*, *Psychological Testing in Children*, *Using Drawings in Assessment and Therapy*), as well as books on child psychotherapy (*Difficult Moments in Child Therapy*) and adolescent depression (*Helping Your Depressed Teenager*).

NORMAN ABELES, Ph.D., is Director of the Clinical Neuropsychological Laboratory and Memory Assessment Center at Michigan State University. Dr. Abeles supervises interns and practicum students, supervises research of graduate students, and conducts extensive research and writing. Dr. Abeles's expertise and research efforts focus on the area of applied aging to help in assisting practitioners in making the transition from full-time work to active retirement. Dr. Abeles has many years of activity in the governance of the American Psychological Association, including a term as president in 1987.

LISE ABRAMS, Ph.D., is Assistant Professor of Psychology at the University of Florida with degrees in cognitive psychology and mathematics. Her research program examines the relationship between memory and language processes in younger and older adults. She specializes in the interaction between memory retrieval and language perception, comprehension, and production. Recent publications are in such journals as *Psychonomic*

Bulletin, Quarterly Journal of Experimental Psychology, and *Research Methods, Instruments, and Computers*.

LEONARD BERKOWITZ, Ph.D., is Professor Emeritus, University of Wisconsin. After graduating from the University of Michigan, he joined the U.S. Air Force Human Resources Center in San Antonio, where he was involved in applying social psychology to real-life situations, then accepted a position at Wisconsin and remained until his retirement. Dr. Berkowitz is well known for his studies of human aggression and helping behavior. He served as editor for *Advances in Experimental Social Psychology*. His books include *Aggression: A Social Psychological Analysis* and *Aggression: Its Causes, Consequences, and Control*.

ELLEN S. BERSCHEID, Ph.D., is Regents Professor of Psychology, University of Minnesota. Her theoretical and empirical work has focused on close interpersonal relationships. Her main interests include problems associated with relationship satisfaction and stability, relationship cognition, and emotional experiences, especially love and sexual desire. She and her research group created and published a measure for relational closeness. Her most recent book is entitled *The Psychology of Interpersonal Relationships*.

BRIAN H. BORNSTEIN, Ph.D., J.D., is Associate Professor, University of Nebraska-Lincoln. He is a member of the law/psychology and cognitive psychology programs, as well as Associate Director of the law/psychology program. Dr. Bornstein's research efforts focus primarily on how juries, especially in civil cases, make decisions and the reliability of eyewitness memory. Additional areas of focus are in applying decision-making principles to everyday judgment tasks, as in medical decision making and distributive justice.

STANLEY BRODSKY, Ph.D., is Professor of Psychology at the University of Alabama. His research interests have focused on the applications of psychology to legal issues and settings and to psychotherapy. His books include *Testifying in Court* and *The Expert Witness*. Other published works have emphasized therapeutic strategies for the treatment of involuntary clients, personality traits of sexual offenders, assessing competence for execution, and serving as an expert witness.

JAMES N. BUTCHER, Ph.D., is Professor Emeritus, University of Minnesota. His research through the years has been in objective personality assessment with focus on the Minnesotat Multiphasic Personality Inventory

(MMPI II) and in developing an adolescent version of the instrument. He has also spent many years on the study of abnormal behavior across cultures. He has developed an objective personality inventory aimed at assessing characteristics of people undergoing psychological treatment. This inventory, the Butcher Treatment Planning Inventory (BTPI), is a self-report instrument that detects problems some people have becoming engaged in psychological therapy.

GUSTAVO CARLO, Ph.D., is Associate Professor in Developmental Psychology, University of Nebraska–Lincoln and a Fellow of the Gallup Research Center. He is an affiliate of the Latino and Latino-American Studies Program, the Child Clinical Psychology Program, and the Center for Children, Families, and the Law at UNL. Dr. Carlo's main scholarly interest is on the individual, parenting, and cultural correlates of positive social and moral behaviors in children and adolescents. He is Associate Editor of the *Journal of Research on Adolescence* and serves on several journal editorial boards.

DANIEL J. CHRISTIE, Ph.D., is Professor of Psychology, Ohio State University. His current research focuses on intercultural sensitivity and bias. He is most enthusiastic about his research model that assesses how students respond to "otherness." Dr. Christie also teaches Introduction to Peace Studies, a course he developed after serving as a visiting professor in Malaysia at the Institute of Technologie Mara. He is past president of the Society for the Study of Peace, Conflict, and Violence of the American Psychological Association and has co-edited a book on peace psychology.

WILLIAM CRAIN, Ph.D., is Professor of Psychology at the City University of New York after graduating from Harvard and the University of Chicago. His research interests include children's play in natural settings and its effect on their emotional and intellectual development. Recent publications include topics on Montessori Life and a textbook, *Theories of Development: Concepts and applications*. He has written extensively as a social activist and has served on local elected organizational boards.

PAT DeLEON, Ph.D., is a clinical psychologist and past president of the American Psychological Association and continues to serve on its board. He has also served as chief of staff for U.S. senator Daniel K. Inouye (D-HI) since 1973. Earning a Ph.D., then a J.D. in law, Dr. DeLeon has been described as a lifelong advocate, motivator, and encourager for the mental health profession. He was one of the primary figures in winning prescription privileges for psychologists and helped social workers secure Medicare reimbursement for outpatient mental health services.

MARILYN T. ERICKSON, Ph.D., is Professor Emerita, Department of Psychology, Virginia Commonwealth University. Her training included graduate work in experimental child clinical psychology at Brown University and the University of Washington. Her books, which emphasized her interests and teaching, include *Behavior Disorders of Children and Adolescents: Assessment, Etiology, and Intervention* and *Child Psychopathology: Assessment, etiology, and treatment*. Dr. Erickson remains active in APA committees in child and youth services.

STEPHEN D. FABICK, Ph.D., is a clinical and consulting psychologist in Birmingham, Michigan, known for his work in conflict resolution, violence prevention, and team building. He is past president of Psychologists for Social Responsibility, an APA organization that uses psychological knowledge and skills to promote peace with justice at the community, national, and international levels. He has published a manual of workshop materials and structured exercises, *Us & Them: The Challenge of Diversity*, for local activist organizations.

JOHN H. FLAVELL, Ph.D., is Professor of Psychology, Stanford University. He is an internationally recognized developmental psychologist elected to the National Academy of Sciences. He has conducted research on the development of role taking and communication skills, metacognition, memory strategies, and children's cognitive maturation. His book *The Developmental Psychology of Jean Piaget* helped introduce the English-speaking world to Piaget's theory and research. He is the recipient of the APA's Distinguished Scientific Contribution, among many other honors and distinctions.

DONELSON R. FORSYTH, Ph.D., serves in an endowed Chair in Ethical Leadership at the University of Richmond after spending many years as a professor of psychology at Virginia Commonwealth University. As a social psychologist, Dr. Forsyth is primarily interested in interpersonal processes. His particular specialties include moral judgment, attribution, and group dynamics, and he has published in many well-known scientific journals, as well as written a half-dozen books on social and group processes, including *Our Social World and Group Dynamics*.

JOHN HARVEY, Ph.D., is Professor of Psychology at the University of Iowa. As a social psychologist, his main research interests have focused on attribution theory, account-making psychological aspects of close relationships, and the social-health-clinical psychology interface. His books include *Embracing Their Memory: Loss and the Social Psychology of Storytelling; Odyssey of the Heart: The Search for Closeness, Intimacy, and Love;* and *Interpersonal Accounts: A Social Psychological Perspective.*

STEPHEN P. HINSHAW, Ph.D., is Professor and Chair of Psychology at University of California–Berkeley. His main interests lie in clinical child psychology and developmental psychopathology. His work includes the diagnostic validity of childhood disorders, the role of peer relationships, identifying subcategories of aggressive behavior, the neuropsychology and neurobiology of externalizing behavior, and the contribution of family factors to acting out and antisocial behavior. Recent publications focus on preadolescent girls with ADHD. He has also published a book entitled *The Years of Silence Are Past: My Father's Life with Bipolar Disorder.*

STEVEN D. HOLLON, Ph.D., is Professor of Psychology, Clinical Science, at Vanderbilt University. His primary interest lies in the etiology and treatment of depression in adults. His work extends from basic psychopathology to prevention and treatment. He is particularly interested in the relative contribution of cognitive and biological processes to depression and how the relative efficacies of psychosocial versus pharmacological interventions compare. A current interest is the prevention of depression, both with respect to its initial onset and subsequent recurrence following successful treatment.

WAYNE HOLTZMAN, Ph.D., Professor Emeritus in Psychology and Education, University of Texas–Austin, served for many years as president of the Hogg Foundation for Mental Health and for several years as dean of the College of Education. He has served as president of the Inter-American Society of Psychology and the International Union of Psychological Science. He currently serves as chairman of the Menninger Clinic's Board of Directors. He has done extensive collaborative research in Mexico, especially in the area of child-rearing, and is author of the *Holtzman Inkblot Technique.*

ELLEN J. LANGER, Ph.D., is Professor of Psychology, Harvard University. Her books written for general and academic readers include *Mindfulness* and *The Power of Mindful Learning* and the forthcoming *Mindful Creativity.* Dr. Langer worked on the illusion of control, aging, decision making, and mindfulness theory in over 200 research articles and six academic books. Her work has led to numerous academic honors, including the Award for Distinguished Contributions to Psychology in the Public Interest from APA and the Gordon Allport Intergroup Relations Prize.

ELLEN LENT, Ph.D. in counseling psychology from Michigan State University, has worked as an assistant dean, in addition to holding positions in training and development, and career planning. She now consults to a high-tech company developing a web-enabled site for career exploration at the high school and college level. She also maintains a private practice specializing in executive coaching. She was recently recognized "Citizen of the Year" within her community for her time and effort in forming *Project Change*, an organization to provide local youth with positive feedback and structure.

ERNEST J. LENZ, Ph.D., MPH, is a retired military psychologist and U.S. Army colonel who now finds himself in the Peace Corps. Through the years, he has been a Special Forces paratrooper, Medical Service Corps officer, a U.S. Army Ranger, Program Manager to the Saudi Arabian National Guard, leader of medical assistance training in El Salvador, Chief of Psychology in Hawaii, and a Consultant for the U.S. Army in Europe. He also spent a year as a Congressional Fellow on Capitol Hill.

BILL LEVIN, Ph.D., a clinical psychologist for over thirty years, began his studies with two eminent personality theorists, Abraham Maslow and George Kelly. He has conducted numerous training programs, written extensively for organizational newsletters, and founded a writers' group. He is currently writing a book, *Sliced Life on Wry: The Personal Evolution Buffet*. His present clinical practice focuses on elderly clients in both outpatient and inpatient settings.

STEVEN R. LOPEZ, Ph.D., is Professor, Psychology, Psychiatry, and Chicana/o Studies, University of California, Los Angeles. His latest research and writings focus on Latino families' reactions to schizophrenia, integrating a cultural perspective in test development, raising standard of multicultural counseling and therapy in working with Latino families, and the social world's impact on mental illness. He has also examined affirmative action guidelines in admissions and clinical stereotypes.

DAVID G. MYERS, Ph.D., is Professor of Psychology at Hope College. Dr. Myers has written articles in more than three dozen magazines, from *Scientific American* to the *Christian Century*, and through fifteen books, including best-selling introduction to psychology and social psychology textbooks, as well as trade titles, such as *What God Has Joined Together? A Christian Case for Gay Marriage* and *Intuition: Its Powers and Perils.*

MICHELLE NEALON-WOODS, Psy.D., is Assistant Professor at the Chicago School of Professional Psychology. She began her career in clinical psychology in Dublin, Ireland, working with adolescents and their families and continues to provide services for this population. Her scholarly interests include the development and improvement of treatment interventions for children and adolescents, particularly focused on improving clinical approaches with diverse populations.

JOAN OFFERLE, Ph.D., has been a licensed psychologist in Texas since 1986 after graduating from an APA-approved counseling psychology program at Virginia Commonwealth University. She has provided counseling services and psychotherapy to adults, college students, the elderly, and couples. She has worked extensively with survivors of trauma and dissociative identity disorders. Relationship issues, bereavement and grief, stress management, and coping with life transitions are other specialty areas she serves.

J. BRUCE OVERMIER, Ph.D., is Professor Emeritus of Psychology at the University of Minnesota and Professor II within the Biological and Medical Psychology Program at the Univesity of Bergen in Norway. Dr. Overmier's research spans specialties of learning, memory, stress, and psychosomatic disorders and their biological substrates. The laboratory animals serve as models for various forms of human dysfunction and the development of therapies (e.g., "learned helplessness" and post-traumatic stress syndrome).

STEVEN PRENTICE-DUNN, Ph.D., is Professor of Psychology at the University of Alabama where he attended both his undergraduate and graduate school education and training. His research interests include interventions to promote preventive health behaviors and social psychology. His published work focuses on the supervision of new instructors, improving teaching methods, applying motivation theory to skin cancer risk, and the effects of coping information and value affirmation on responses to perceived health threats.

THOMAS R. PROHASKA, Ph.D., is Professor, School of Public Health, University of Illinois–Chicago. His research focuses on coping with chronic illness, self-care, doctor/patient interaction, and community interventions with older adults. Teaching interests include gerontological health, illness behavior, and public health and aging. Publications have emphasized physical activity, exercise benefits, behavioral counseling, health and illness behavior in the elderly, and health promotion.

JULIAN RAPPAPORT, Ph.D., is Professor Emeritus, University of Illinois. His interests span the broad domain of community psychology, a field he first conceptualized with the publication of *Community Psychology: Values, research and action* and more recently with the *Handbook of Community Psychology*. His research has emphasized juvenile justice, prevention and empowerment, self- and mutual help, and school consultation and organization with poor and minority children.

FRANK H. RATH JR., Ph.D., has been director of army internship programs and a teaching consultant to Walter Reed Army Medical Center. He served more than twenty-three years' active duty, including one year in Vietnam before becoming a psychologist and two tours in Germany as an army psychologist. Dr. Rath has also maintained a private practice, has been a consultant to the U.S. Department of State, and was clinical associate professor at the University of Maryland Medical School.

JUDITH RODIN, Ph.D., is President of the Rockefeller Foundation. She is the first woman to lead the foundation, which works to help ensure that the benefits of globalization are shared more equitably. Dr. Rodin is former president of the University of Pennsylvania, where she spent a decade of service. Previously, Dr. Rodin was on the faculty of Yale University and served as provost. She also has authored or coauthored eleven books in health psychology and behavioral medicine.

ESTHER D. ROTHBLUM, Ph.D., is Professor of Women's Studies at San Diego State University and past Professor of Psychology at the University of Vermont. Her research and writing have focused on lesbian relationships and mental health, and she is editor of the *Journal of Lesbian Studies*. She has edited over twenty books, including *Preventing Heterosexism and Homophobia* and *Lesbians in Academia*.

M. BREWSTER SMITH, Ph.D., is Professor Emeritus, University of California at Santa Cruz. He conducted groundbreaking work on the ways people's opinions are influenced by their strategies for coping with the world, their social relations, and their inner conflicts. He has also drawn on psychological research to suggest ways to reduce threats of nuclear war. Dr. Smith served as an expert witness, testifying against school segregation in *Brown v. the Board of Education*.

ROBERT J. STERNBERG, Ph.D., is IBM Professor of Psychology and Education at Yale University. His major contributions include the triarchic theory of human intelligence and other influential theories and books related to creativity, intelligence, thinking styles, and education. His discoveries have influenced cognitive science and have resulted in the rethinking of conventional methods of evaluating an individual's intelligence.

HARRY C. TRIANDIS, Ph.D., is Professor Emeritus, University of Illinois. A pioneer in cross-cultural psychology, Dr. Triandis has addressed fundamental problems of how people in different societies define their self-concept and relate to others. His early research established models for preparing workers to adjust to other cultures. This work established training programs on how minority group members adjust to society. He is the author of *Individualism and Collectivism*.